Culture and Enterprise

What is the animating "spirit" behind what may appear to be the coldly calculating world of markets and business enterprise? Though often mathematically modeled in dry terms, markets can be looked at instead as meaningful domains of human activity. To economists, markets have been seen as nothing but objective "forces" or allocation "mechanisms." This book, however, argues that they can be seen as involving the human spirit, personal expression and moral commitments. It presents the view that markets are not so much things that need to be measured as meanings that need to be narrated and interpreted.

The aim of this book is to introduce two scholarly fields to one another, economics and cultural studies, in order to pose the question: How does culture matter to the economy? When we look at the economy as a legitimate domain of culture it transforms our understanding of the nature of business life. By viewing markets as an integral part of our culture, filled with the drama of human creativity, we might begin to better appreciate their role in the world.

Don Lavoie is the David H. and Charles G. Koch Professor of Economics at the School of Public Policy, George Mason University. His previous publications include *Rivalry and Central Planning*, *National Economic Planning: What is Left?* and *Economics and Hermeneutics*.

Emily Chamlee-Wright is Associate Professor of Economics and Management at Beloit College. She is the author of *The Cultural Foundations of Economic Development: Urban Female Entrepreneurship in Ghana*.

Routledge Studies in the Modern World Economy

Culture and Enterprise

The development, representation and morality of business

Don Lavoie and Emily Chamlee-Wright

A Cato Institute Book

London and New York

First published 2000 by Routledge
11 New Fetter Lane, London EC4P 4EE

Simultaneously published in the USA and Canada
by Routledge
29 West 35th Street, New York, NY 10001

Routledge is an imprint of the Taylor & Francis Group

© 2000 The Cato Institute

Typeset in Garamond by
MHL Typesetting Ltd, Coventry
Printed and bound in Great Britain by
Clays Ltd, St Ives plc

British Library Cataloguing in Publication Data
A catalogue record for this book is available from the British Library

Library of Congress Cataloging-in-Publication Data

Lavoie, Don, 1951–
    Culture and enterprise: the development, representation, and morality
    of business/Don Lavoie and Emily Chamlee-Wright
      p. cm.
    Includes bibliographical reference and index
    1. Economic development – Social aspects. 2. Culture.
    3. Business ethics. I. Chamlee-Wright, Emily, 1966– II. Title.

  HD75.I.38.2000
  306.3–dc21   00-042489

ISBN 0-415-23358-5 (hbk)
ISBN 0-415-23359-3 (pbk)

To Mary and Brian,
for your gifts of love, friendship,
and laughter

Contents

1 Introduction

> A public sphere that functions politically requires more than the institutional guarantees of the constitutional state; it also needs the supportive spirit of cultural traditions and patterns of socialization, of the political culture, of a populace accustomed to freedom.
>
> Jürgen Habermas (1992a: 453)

The economy, just like the democratic polity, requires more than the institutional guarantees of the constitutional state. Economists have had much of value to say about business decision-making, about the efficiency conditions for the success of individual business enterprises, and about the material and institutional conditions that are conducive to economic prosperity, but rarely do they pay attention to the question of culture. Yet it may well be that it is attention to this more "spiritual" realm that will most help us to understand the workings of the economy.

The events over the past decade in the former soviet sphere illustrate well the fact that neither of the fundamental components of a free society, neither its relatively democratic political character nor its relatively entrepreneurial economic environment, can emerge without what Jürgen Habermas calls the "supportive spirit of cultural traditions and patterns of socialization." An active democratic participation in the public sphere does not arise automatically upon the declaration of the overthrow of a dictator. A flourishing market economy does not automatically arise from the ashes of a centrally planned economy the moment somebody declares the end of communism and the institution of a formal system of property rights. Political and economic freedom is not simply the absence of government controls over the economy and of dictatorial authority. It involves the emergence of alternative and more fragmented notions of "authority" in which participants in effect have to earn the always partial authority they have. It depends on the active participation in the polity and in the economy by diverse people who exercise their own initiative.

1.1 The spirit of enterprise

What is the "spirit" of business enterprise? What is the animating spirit behind what may appear to be the coldly calculating world of markets and business competition? Though markets are often described and mathematically modeled in dry, spiritless terms, markets could be looked at instead as meaningful domains of human activity. From the perspective of mainstream economics, markets are nothing but objective "forces" or reasonably efficient allocation "mechanisms," but they are not seen as meaningful elements of culture.

Market activity and business life need not be thought of as merely physical, as something that needs to be measured or simulated on a computer. They can also be thought of as spiritual, in the sense that they involve the human spirit, personal expression, values, principles, moral commitments. They are not so much things that need to be measured as meanings that need to be narrated and interpreted.

The market is often described (by Habermas, for example) as if it represented some sort of inhuman system intruding upon human affairs, sometimes "colonizing" our life-world and forcing us to work around it. But it can be understood to be a legitimate part of our larger cultural existence, not some sort of alien intrusion into it. Business decision-making, though it is often described as a mechanical optimization of quantitative variables, can instead be seen as the locus of creativity and of moral responsibility. The business world may often be associated with hierarchical relationships and bureaucratic routine, but it is also the site of spirited human dramas, a domain in which noble ideals can be pursued and uplifting values can be defended. Though our popular culture may have a tendency to depict the business world as a gray realm of dubious moral standing, it can also be seen as fully a part of the human world, with all the vices and virtues of other domains of life.

1.2 The study both of markets and culture

The point of this book is to reframe the question of the relationship between cultural and economic processes. The question is exceedingly important but it has not, for the most part, been adequately posed, much less answered. We want to indicate how we think the issue needs to be framed if pursuing it is to yield useful insight. To us the people who clearly *ought* to be asking this question are scholars from the fields of economics and cultural studies, and, since each lacks important strengths of the other, they ought to be working together on it.

The over-separation of the social science disciplines from one another and from the humanities have obscured our ability to comprehend the fundamental nature of business enterprise and market processes. It may seem almost too obvious to ask what culture has to do with economic development, or how popular images of business that prevail in the culture might influence the way people view business enterprise, or how understanding the moral values in the culture may be relevant to the study of business decision-making. But seemingly obvious questions such as these are exceedingly difficult to pose at an advanced level of scholarship today.

The reason is that the two fields of study that should have the most to say about these issues do not speak the same language. Specialized scholarship in the study of culture rarely comes into any useful contact with specialized scholarship in the study of markets and business enterprise in addressing questions such as these. At economics departments scant attention is paid to the ways economic decisions are made in a larger ethical context that is shaped by culture, or the ways in which culture can shape economic development. At business schools though one can find frequent references to "corporate culture," the analysis of culture is usually so thin that it would not be taken seriously by most scholars in the humanities. At English, anthropology, sociology, and history departments, though, where serious work on culture is often done, little attention is paid to the workings of the business world, for example, to the culture of business organizations, except when traditional Marxist scholars simply demonize business as inherently exploitative and immoral. We want to suggest that a better understanding of the economy and business life can result from *taking seriously* the role of culture in economic processes.

Taking these ideas seriously means engaging in a respectful dialogue with some of the leading scholarly work from both the discipline of economics and that of cultural studies. Indeed, it means trying to come to an in-depth understanding of the culture of one another's scholarly traditions. The authors of this monograph are trained within, and have no doubt imbued much of the culture of, the field of economics, a field that is notorious for its mishandling of interdisciplinary scholarship. When economists venture into foreign disciplinary terrain, they tend either to merely dabble in the field's issues at a superficial level, which might be called tourism, or to try to aggressively take over the issues of the field on their own terms, which has come to be called economic imperialism.

Tourism is the attitude of the brief visitor who never really learns a culture because he stays in the hotels and not in the villages among the people, who sees the official sights that are on the route of the tour bus, and hears the accounts of the guides, conveniently translated into his own language, but never gets out and experiences everyday life with the people. An example of a disciplinary tourist is the economist who reads a book about cultural studies, not a work within the field written in its native tongue, and decides on what it is all about from within the safety of his own disciplinary framework.

Imperialism involves more contact with "the natives" but since the contact is violent it is no less apt to result in misunderstanding. Some effort is made to identify the issues the invaded discipline is grappling with, but the discipline's own traditions for addressing the issues are dismissed as the product of primitives, of pre-scientific, semi-civilized peoples. The Imperial Discipline is brought in as the Experts who will solve the natives' problems for them by applying Modern Science and Technique.

One of the insights of cultural studies is that productive encounters between diverse cultures demand that each side attempt to learn the language of the other, that each open itself to the possible truths of the other perspective. This requires more extended contact than is possible on a tour, but also a radically different kind of contact than occurs in colonial conquest. It requires an attitude of receptivity, an honest attempt to find the enduring qualities in the other's ideas and activities. It requires that one risk one's own point of view against the truth-claims of the other. This is as true of encounters between academic cultures as of any other.

There is no question but that battles between traditional left- and right-wing ideology have exacerbated the communicative difficulties here. Cultural studies scholars are apt to be dismissed by many economists as crazy leftists, and economists are apt to be dismissed by many cultural studies scholars as crazy right-wingers. The left accuses the right of a naive faith that "markets" – understood as some kind of objective force unrelated to human purposes or democratic politics – will solve all our problems. The right accuses the left of a naive faith that "politics" – understood as good people in government who will follow the democratic will of the people – will solve all our problems. And most folks find some truth in both accusations, and increasingly reject both sides as naive.

But the real issue here is not the old ideological stalemates between the left and the right. What divides the discourse about markets and culture even more than policy conclusions are diverse methodological proclivities and the professionalization and mutual isolation of the various disciplines. Scholars in the more humanities-oriented disciplines that focus on philosophical, historical and literary modes of investigation are genuinely deepening our understanding of culture, but have tended to consider markets to be a topic that belongs to the field of economics, or to the various business disciplines like marketing, and a matter outside their domain of expertise. Those in economics who deploy more social-scientific modes of investigation such as mathematical modeling and statistical analyses, speak an utterly different language, and see little scope to apply their analytical tools to the concept of culture. If asked why they pay no attention to culture, economists could revert to the excuse that it is simply not in their job description. It is not within the purview of economics as a profession to judge the contents or merits of an individual's preferences, so culture, which forms these preferences, falls out of the domain of economic inquiry.

Our discourse has been damaged not only by the fact that the economists and the various students of culture, because of their long-standing *differences*, tend to be incapable of listening to one another. Perhaps more serious have been the consequences of the underlying *agreements* between them. One issue they agree about is that culture and market processes are utterly distinct kinds of phenomena. The attitudes toward markets among non-economists range from those who find economics boring and degrading, and ignore markets altogether, to those who consider economics important but find markets to be an invasive force, distorting and corrupting culture. Economists have insisted on analyzing markets as universal causal mechanisms, systems that are presumed to be utterly indifferent to culture. They tend to view markets as positively beneficial, but see the benefits as resulting from "equilibrating tendencies" that are propelled by the actions of atomistic, acultural individuals.

That is, the economists take markets seriously but see culture as irrelevant to economic performance, while the others take culture seriously but see markets as uninteresting or evil. Rarely does one find any systematic analysis of the relevance culture has for markets. Even those economists who do see the important role social institutions play in the economic process (for example, North 1989, 1990, 1994; Alchian and Demsetz 1973; Bauer 1954, 1984; and Harriss *et al.* 1995) do not focus on the cultural foundations which give rise to and maintain those social institutions.

What is needed is a genuine engagement between the perspectives of cultural studies and economics, not only with one another's issues, but also with one another's analytical tools and scholarly standards. At the present time there is such a chasm between the disciplinary cultures of economics and cultural studies that any early effort to open up communication is fraught with the dangers of misunderstanding. This study is intended to initiate a process of mutual engagement between the fields of economics and cultural studies in the hopes that some of the valid and useful achievements of each can become known to the other.

1.3 Civil society and cultural studies

There are signs that the old ideological positions of the left and right and the old methodological boundaries separating economics from the humanities are weakening. In the aftermath of the collapse of soviet socialism and the decline of the cold war's left/right rhetoric, as well as other intellectual trans-formations which we will discuss, there may now be an opportunity to develop a better understanding of the mutual relationships between cultural and market processes.

The idea of civil society is becoming a promising one from the point of view of rejuvenating social theory. The fundamental ideas of thinkers as diverse as Jürgen Habermas and Friedrich Hayek can be seen to share a fundamental concern over the nature of civil society. Contemporary discussions of civil society, and the related issues of carving out a "public space" for a non-coercive politics, are beginning to breathe fresh life into social and political thought. (See for example, Calhoun 1992; Putnam 1993; Havel 1992.) Intellectual traditions that arise out of very diverse roots are reconceiving themselves and coming into connection with one another over the notion of civil society.

A crucial issue that is driving this reconfiguration is culture. Elements of what used to be called the right – for example the civic republicanism tradition within conservatism and the Austrian school economists within libertarian and classical liberal thought – are coming to appreciate the cultural underpinnings of a free society, and are emancipating their own arguments from a narrow focus on the efficiency of markets. Meanwhile elements of what used to be called the left – especially several branches of the whole new field that is being called "cultural studies" – are coming to appreciate the cultural underpinnings of democracy, and emancipating themselves from a narrow faith in governmental solutions to social problems.

The discussion of democracy and the ideal of the public sphere in the contemporary Frankfurt School of critical theory, for example, explores what it means to form a free society. This literature tries to show how the separate Enlightenment ideals of reason and freedom each need to be reinterpreted, and how when this is done they are found to be intimately related to one another. The Enlightenment liberals loved reason, but too often misunderstood it to be what Habermas calls instrumental reason. The Enlightenment celebrated individual rights, but too often based them on natural law arguments that have not stood up well to contemporary critique. And it did not seem to have a clear notion of the way reason and freedom are related to one another. For some contributors to critical theory, the idea of reasoning together in a context of mutual respect, protected by a certain domain of rights, is the very core of what we should mean by a democratic polity.

Habermas understands a democratic polity as a dialogical process, as the explicit public discourse about our common concerns, and examines the underlying conditions, such as openness to other perspectives, that are necessary for effective dialogue. Hayek and the Austrian School understand a free market as a similar dialogical process, as the implicit "discourse" of diverse market experiments in open competitive interplay. Both are talking about civil society. It could be argued that critical theory is trying to do for politics what the Austrian School is trying to do for economics: conceive of its central phenomena as unintended results of social learning processes. There may be an entrepreneurial opportunity for some intellectual gains from trade here. There may be a chance for an exciting renewal of our stalemated ideological discourses.

But the legacy of distrust that has divided our social thought is profound, and will make any effort of renewal extraordinarily difficult. The latest obstacles to understanding have been the battles in academia over Political Correctness. It is undeniable that elements of the left have often been guilty of promoting a PC censorship mentality, for which they have been harshly criticized by many prominent leftists and contributors to cultural studies (see Jay and Graff 1995; Gitlin 1995; Said 1993). But we find equally problematic the sweeping condemnations that elements of the right – we will call them the cultural conservatives – have often made of the whole of academia, or of whole scholarly traditions within academia.

Among the intellectual currents that such cultural conservatives as Martin Anderson (1992), Dinesh D'Souza (1991), and others have targeted is the cultural studies literature, which we will contend in fact holds great promise for renewing our social thought. They equate cultural studies with political correctness, and are alarmed at what they take to be its agenda, a wholesale critique of traditional American values, and a rejection of the great works of literature. What cultural conservatives condemn as a thinly disguised politicization of literature by "tenured radicals," we will describe as, on the contrary, a powerful current of serious scholarly research into the nature of democracy. What they presume is a continuation of the old ideology of the left, we see as constituting a major turn in radical thought that opens the door for a fundamental reconsideration of the nature of markets.

Contrary to the caricatures made by the anti-PC conservatives, the left today is anything but a unified collective of political correctness police. Long before the collapse of the soviet system most leftists had abandoned their ill-placed faith in centralized planning, and after the collapse there seems to be an acceleration of its tendencies to develop its democratic and decentralized ideals. Within the cultural studies tradition are some of the most eloquent defenders of individual rights, of the importance of respecting difference, of the value of free speech and open discourse. There is more questioning today of the orthodoxies of traditional Marxism within cultural studies than ever before in academia. There is more challenging of the cultural elitism of the old left, and more openness to populist movements, and to popular culture than ever before. There is more questioning of the New Class of bureaucrats and the failure of the welfare state than one finds in most conservative literature.

It is true that issues that the media labels leftist, or politically correct – concerns over issues of gender, race, class, and sexual orientation – are central to the cultural studies literature, and that issues labelled conservative, such as marginal tax rates or the deregulation of financial markets, are not. But the whole way many cultural studies scholars are thinking about the "leftist" issues is changing. Solutions to gender bias, for example, are not automatically sought in government programs to punish businesses who discriminate, but are often sought through nongovernmental means within the culture itself.

Cultural studies is one of the scholarly movements that is most closely affiliated with the loose term "post-modernism." The notion of the post-modern is deployed as a broad cultural symbol, sometimes signaling styles in architecture, or poetry, sometimes pointing to the information age. It has been described as a philosophy that has an affinity with the Internet and technological developments toward hypertext (see for example, Landow 1992; Lanham 1995). The post-modern world is one where products are made of bits instead of molecules, where "image is everything," where everything is like a text, and all texts are interconnected. The characteristic mode of post-modernism is irony, and especially the ironies surrounding self-referentiality.

The world, it says, is increasingly fragmented, disunified, free-floating, ungrounded.

For our purposes here, what is of interest is post-modernism's scholarly contributions to our understanding of knowledge. Its various strands, in different ways, identify important limitations in the "modernistic" thinking that dominates economics and much of the rest of the social sciences (we will discuss modernism further in the next chapter). Modernistic thinking is seen as static, as oriented toward centralized control, as focussed on forcing things into universal categories and smoothing over differences, as preoccupied with average phenomena and insufficiently attentive to the margins.

Cultural studies represents the culmination of some of the most sophisticated strands of post-modern social thought that have been coming from the disciplines of philosophy, literary criticism, anthropology and the interpretive elements of the other social sciences. These strands are being woven together into an impressive interdisciplinary field of study in its own right. Among the intellectual traditions it builds upon are the leading developments in continental philosophy, including contemporary work in phenomenology and hermeneutics stemming from the work of Martin Heidegger and Hans-Georg Gadamer, the philosophy of deconstruction from the work of Jacques Derrida and his followers, and Michel Foucault's genealogical approach to history. The leading branches of contemporary Marxism and feminism are part of the movement, as well as most of the current work in literary studies. (Useful introductions to the field are Brantlinger 1990; Davis and Schleiffer 1989; During 1993b; Fox and Lears 1993; Grossberg *et al.* 1992; Leitch 1988; Makaryk 1993; Munch and Smelser 1992; Sahlins 1976; Sarup 1989; Selden 1989; and Warnke 1987.)

One of the best short descriptions of the cultural studies field we have seen was written by Mark Jacobs (1994):

> Across an entire range of disciplines, scholars are embracing new conceptions of culture and new methods for its study. No longer do we contrast culture with structure; rather we emphasize that culture exists in intimate relation with structure. We now tend to view culture as a context rather than a force; a "tool kit" of habits, skills, and styles from which people construct strategies of action in everyday life, rather than a set of ultimate values; a space of contestation and change rather than a cybernetic mechanism of equilibrium-seeking and pattern maintenance.
>
> In sociology, history, political science, and economics, scholars are bringing culture (no longer the exclusive province of anthropology) into their analyses, and seizing the "interpretive turn" in doing so; literary critics recognize the intersubjective nature of cultural processes, turning to the social sciences to help explain them. Social science explicitly draws on literary criticism in its concern with narrativity, while literary criticism draws on social science in its concern with the embeddedness of texts in economic, political, and social practices. Despite the significant difference

between ethnographic "thick description" and literary criticism – the one focused on social interaction, the other focused on texts – both involve constructing and then analyzing detailed, descriptive representations of cultural objects.

Hence the emergence of Cultural Studies as an attempt to link the social sciences and the humanities, combining methods of interpretation and explanation to explore the dynamics of intention and reception in the production, distribution, and consumption of cultural objects in their interactional and societal contexts.

Although much of the cultural studies literature either shows no ideological orientation, or evidences a distinctively leftist slant, there is also a strong attitude of decentralization and anti-authoritarianism throughout the literature which, though clearly critical of modern liberalism, resonates in many ways with classical liberalism. The resonance is even stronger when one considers the post-modernist strands of the contemporary classical liberal and libertarian traditions. (We have in mind the sort of libertarianism that is being developed in the journal *Critical Review*. See for example Beiner 1993; Beito 1990; diZerega 1989; Johnson 1990; Madison 1988, 1989, 1990a, 1991b; McCloskey 1991, 1997; Minogue 1989; Murphy 1995; Neaman 1988; Palmer 1991b; Prychitko 1990b; Schrag 1991; Sciabarra 1987; Taylor 1994.) Many of the leading contributors to cultural studies, such as Habermas, Edward Said (1983), or Albrecht Wellmer (1991), articulate a critique of traditional leftist ideology in a manner that leaves room for reconciliation with a classical liberal, market-oriented policy approach.

Like liberalism, cultural studies celebrates diversity, but unlike many modern liberals, it does not see its tolerance as flowing from an arm's length disinterestedness, but on the contrary advocates immersion into cultural specifics, and declares its interests forthrightly, refusing to pretend that it can or should aspire to value-neutrality. Like conservatism, it attacks the liberal establishment's pretense of objectivity, and celebrates the importance of values. But unlike conservatism it is not prepared to accept that there exists a uniform standard – the good old-fashioned values of white-bread, bourgeois, American culture – that can be deployed to judge good and bad values. Some cultural conservatives try to invent, out of the rich variety of American culture, a homogeneous middle-class culture, the "silent majority," and try to blame our problems on the erosion of these particular values. Cultural studies makes an important move as it challenges the myth of a single national culture. By emphasizing the different ways of seeing the diverse and conflicting strands within a society's cultural process, cultural studies recognizes the heterogeneous voices within the discourse about values.

This is not to suggest that no common ground need exist in a discourse regarding values. Indeed, successful dialogue requires that the participants agree, either tacitly or consciously, to some rules of the game. A free and open discussion of religion, for example, depends upon the assurance that converts will be won through persuasion, not coercion. Individual rights serve as the common ground in this case. Only by adhering to such rules of the game is a genuine dialogue even possible. Here again, we see the similarities and differences among classical liberalism and cultural studies. Both recognize the necessity for individual rights and freedom of expression. Yet, while classical liberals have traditionally appealed to rights as objective benchmarks, cultural studies recognizes that the rights governing the interaction among individuals are themselves the outcome of a discursive process which takes place in a particular cultural context. This is not to suggest that rights are arbitrary, or to lessen the importance they play in the maintenance of the social order, but rather to illustrate the pervasive influence of culture at all levels.

It is not only from the left that we are finding a renewed attention to the role of culture and values in society. A growing number of economists reject the model of atomistic individualism and refuse to treat market phenomena as external to politics and culture. The notion of community is becoming an important issue for both conservative and radical political thought. The revival of the southern civic republican tradition in American political thought, for example, in the works of Genovese (1994), Wilson (1981), and Reed (1986, 1995), celebrates the notion of community in terms many on the left would find congenial. Without soviet communism to bring out the worst militaristic tendencies of the right wing, elements of it are turning in very different directions, with which many on the left would find common ground.

But the renewal of our social thought is just beginning. So far very little has been done to illuminate the cultural aspects of market institutions. For the renewal to continue it is vital that we deepen our awareness of the way cultural processes relate to economic processes.

1.4   The development, representation, and morality of business

The next two chapters set the stage by elaborating on the idea of culture and its relationship to economic issues. The field of cultural studies has much to offer to the student of economic processes. We begin by trying in Chapter 2 to sum up in some detail what cultural studies has to tell us about what culture is, how it changes, and how it should be studied. Chapter 3 then asks whether this sort of study is compatible with economics, and if so, which ways of thinking about economics are most conducive to fitting with and contributing to what cultural studies has to say. These two bodies of literature have yet to have been, as they say, properly introduced. It seems to us there is much for each side to learn from the other.

The key question of this book is how culture matters to the economic system. Each of these bodies of literature has, for different reasons, largely failed so far to get at the question. Economics suffers from methodological blinders that keep it from saying much useful about culture, and that even obstruct its ability to understand markets. Cultural studies corrects for some of these methodological problems, but has a few serious problems of its own which have kept it from contributing much to the issue.

Although we will be quite critical of both of these literatures, our purpose is ultimately to draw from each to correct for biases of the other. From economics can be found the work of the Austrian school, which has made valuable contributions to the theory of entrepreneurship (See Mises 1949; Kirzner 1973, 1979, 1985, 1992; Vaughn 1993), and which holds the potential of bringing cultural issues into its analysis. From cultural studies can be found researchers who are beginning to take economic processes seriously (see Bourdieu 1977; Douglas and Isherwood 1979; Gudeman 1986; Madison 1990b, 1991a; Prendergast 1986; Robben 1989). If such scholars as these can get together, there is some reason to be hopeful. The way toward an understanding of the cultural foundations of a prosperous society requires that much of what has been learned by economists about markets and entrepreneurship, and by cultural studies theorists about language and identity, be integrated with one another.

It makes a difference for our understanding of the development, representation, and morality of business life when we look at it as a legitimate domain of meaningful culture. It makes a difference for the way we conceive of the *development* of business. We will argue in Chapter 4 that the issue of economic development, the entrepreneurial process through which the economy grows, is approached very differently when one pays attention to the cultural values relevant to business enterprise. Economic prosperity, we will argue, depends as much upon a certain "enterprising spirit," a set of values, attitudes, aspirations, and orientations in the culture, as it does upon any so-called objective or material conditions of the society. The first half of the chapter presents a critique of cross-national cultural comparisons as the way to ask useful questions about the role of culture in economic change. The question of how culture may be more or less conducive to economic prosperity is too culture-specific to be usefully answered in the abstract, and at the coarse aggregative level of national GDP comparisons. We think that one can shed more light on the way culture can be conducive to economic prosperity by going for the finer granularity of detailed ethnographic case studies. The latter half of the chapter takes a look at some research that examines the entrepreneurial spirit in a few cultural contexts in American and East Asian societies. We find that entrepreneurship manifests itself in strikingly different modes of behavior in different cultures.

When we look at business life as a legitimate domain of meaningful culture, it makes a difference in the way the *representation* of the world of business gets done in our culture. What shapes a society's images of the entrepreneur, and what do those images shape? As the popular culture movement in cultural studies demonstrates, images developed in "the culture industry" are profoundly important influences over a society's system of beliefs. Chapter 5 examines the way American popular culture depicts, reflects, is shaped by, and shapes public attitudes toward markets and business enterprise. That is, we take a look at how the media, television and movies, reproduce, circulate and create the images we have of the nature of business enterprise, market relationships, and government policy. The influence exerted by popular culture is a complex one. Cultural studies has shown the capacity of consumers in market relationships to "read against the grain," to insist upon their own meanings, and often to resist the dominant attitudes of the culture. Thus Chapter 5 elaborates on the way in which *consumers* in a market society cannot be treated as helpless puppets of Madison Avenue but need to be seen as conscious agents in their own right.

Chapter 6 goes on to suggest that cultural studies should begin similarly to rethink the capacity of *producers* within the domain of business enterprise to be active moral agents, exerting their own points of view, sometimes against the dominant views. When we look at business life as a legitimate domain of meaningful culture, it makes a difference for the way the *morality* of the world of business is understood. Too often cultural studies of the business world (see for example, Jackall 1988) suggest that corporate life is nothing but an arena for back-room political dealings and moral compromises. Cultural studies scholarship depicts businesses co-opting admirable social causes (see for example, Frank and Weiland 1997) but businesses never seem genuinely to advance them.

Mainstream economics, for its part, tends to depict the business agent as an amoral mechanism that simply responds to market forces. A business person who obeys the law is neither a hero nor a villain, he is only carrying out the will of the stockholders, or ultimately the will of the consumer, and so is outside of the realm of moral judgment. We would like to challenge both the cultural studies stereotype of the businessman as villain, and the economists' image of the business agent as an optimizing robot. We would like to take seriously the ethical dimension of business life, and the possibilities for producers in the market economy to act in a morally admirable way.

Culture is a whole orientation to the world, a way of living that necessarily involves ethical choices. Economists have tended to argue that the business manager's behavior should not be judged other than on the criterion of whether he is obeying the law and serving the stockholders by making a profit. Indeed the formal models seem to leave no room for discretion, the business decision-maker either does what the market tells her to, or gets eliminated. The business ethics literature, however, keeps finding real-world moral dilemmas that managers encounter in everyday life.

In all these dimensions of culture, its role in our understanding of economic development, its influence through its representation of business life in popular film and other media on the values and beliefs of market participants, and its relevance to the morality of business, the cultural studies way of thinking about culture corrects for weaknesses in what economists have had to say about the economy. In particular, the insistence by cultural studies scholars on paying attention to difference, to the heterogeneous elements of dynamic cultural processes, has been a welcome corrective to the tendency of modern social sciences including economics to aggregate and average out all the diversity, and to overemphasize the permanent structures at the expense of the flexible dynamics of decentralized change.

2 What is culture and why does it matter?

For Hegel, and for many of his contemporaries, the Greek polis had always been an exemplary model for the political institutionalization of freedom. At the same time, the Greek polis provided him with a model for illustrating his thesis that political freedom can be real only as a form of ethical life (*Sittlichkeit*). Hegel used the term "ethical life" to characterize the normative structure of an intersubjective form of life. The ethical life of a people – in contrast to what Hegel called "morality"– is inseparable from its institutions, its collective interpretations of the world, its ways of self-understanding, its customs, traditions, and values.

Albrecht Wellmer (1991: 232)

Culture is a framework of meaning, an *aspect* of virtually any causal factor one might identify, not a separate causal factor of its own. It is the background that provides the linguistic framework with which we understand the world around us. But this particular aspect of all the political, sociological, and economic factors that drive social change has been neglected in the age of positivistic social science, and is in need of emphasis. Too eager to plot the trajectories of causal mechanisms, the social scientists paid little attention to the plot lines of the agent's own stories. They paid too little attention to figuring out what things meant to the agents involved, to gaining close, ethnographic contact with the actors, to attending to the subtleties of interpretation in "reading" what is going on in complex social processes. As many social scientists from political theory to sociology are finding, the causal processes they are identifying as important factors in social change all point back to culture.

Of all the social sciences, economics is the one that most desperately needs to pay more attention to the cultural aspects of what it studies. The images and symbolic messages we receive and send through culture profoundly shape the way we think about such issues as the proper role for government, the rule of law, contractual obligations, professional ethics, private property rights, and the monetary order. These ways of thinking, by setting the framework within which all the political and economic interactions will take place, can be viewed as crucial elements underlying the quality of our lives in the workplace, the place the world of business enterprise occupies in our larger social existence, and the overall prospects for the expansion of economic wealth.

A culture is shaped by and in turn shapes the pervasive meanings, dispositions, and images that are inscribed in it through the metaphors we use and the stories we tell. The plots of popular movies convey images of the world of business enterprise which influence that world, and the economics courses MBA students take convey certain attitudes about ethical responsibility that influence their behavior in that world. Institutions critical to social progress, including economic prosperity, depend upon the interpretive framework culture provides.

Take, for example, the issue we will come to in Chapter 4: What are the main contributors to economic prosperity? A substantial and rather persuasive thesis to be found throughout the 200 year literature of economics is that a healthy economy requires relatively widespread allegiance to certain principles of "civil society," principles which specify the boundaries of socially legitimated actions. Yet, civil society and the institutions so necessary to the market economy must find legitimization within the cultural context. Contractual obligation, private property rights, and the justice system cannot function in a society without a commonly held notion of what a contract actually is, what can and cannot legitimately be bought and sold, and what constitutes justice.

Or take the case of business ethics which we will address in Chapter 6. What is taken to be acceptable ethical behavior in business depends completely on the prevailing values of the culture. A sophisticated credit market cannot even get started without a culture in which a sufficient degree of honesty prevails. Here too, the issues the study of economics and business point to suggest the importance of culture throughout economic life.

Another large and persuasive body of writing to be found among scholars all across the humanities – that is, the 20 year literature of the interdisciplinary field called cultural studies – has deepened our understanding of just what sort of thing a society's cultural process is. It sheds light on the question of how we can understand what drives a society's allegiance to any body of beliefs. Underneath a prosperous society's commitment to rules of just and honest conduct can be found an evolving culture that identifies for most people what constitutes admirable and ethical action, and what constitutes objectionable behavior. Underneath the apparently purely calculative decisions of business can be found the cultural realm where human values and moral responsibility are relevant. The field of cultural studies is a sincere effort to understand particular cultures and subcultures, and how they change, to better appreciate what is involved in the "reading" of a culture and its artifacts.

2.1 Culture as context: from the arts to morality

Culture may be understood in several distinct but closely related senses. Cultural anthropologists, historians and interpretive sociologists tend to see it as a framework of meaning that provides the context within which people understand the world around them. In everyday language, and in literary theory and the humanities, the word is most often taken to refer more specifically to the arts: the "culture" section of the newspaper is where you find reviews of movies and novels. Still other uses of the word stress the ethical and moral attitudes of a society, for example, in the way discussions of business ethics deal with the morals prevalent in a "corporate culture." There have been tendencies for the social sciences and the arts artificially to separate themselves, divvying up the world into the study of objective truth and subjective beauty, and leaving issues of ethics outside of both. Cultural studies refuses to play by these rules, and brings in, under the rubric of culture, a full range of social issues, bearing on all aspects of our everyday lives. We will try to show that each of these senses of the term is importantly related to the world of business enterprise.

The ambiguity among these various meanings of culture should be taken as a productive sort of ambiguity, signalling an important overlap of connotations of the word "culture" in *our* culture. There may be a tendency for traditional sociologists to define culture as context in a way that pays no particular attention to the arts, and a tendency for traditional literary theorists to treat culture exclusively as a matter of interpreting artistic expression, as if this were disconnected from everyday life. What makes the field of cultural studies different in part is that it deliberately fuzzes up that dubious distinction, showing that culture plays a crucial role in shaping our mental models, our moral standards, our aesthetic sensibilities, and in general, the contexts that give meaning to our lives.

All of these various connotations of the word "culture" have a common connection to the conception of culture as a framework of meaning. Suppose we were to relate carefully the details of a ritual dance; laying out every step and every sequence. If that is all we have done, we really have not said much, if anything, about the culture of the people who practice the ritual. On the other hand, if we were also to relate how the ritual fits into the lives of the people who practice it, in other words, what *meaning* the ritual has for the people who practice it, we have said much about the culture of the people. It is in this sense that we can also call the rituals, the art, and the moral systems of a people culture, not simply as objects or rules, but as part of the framework of meaning that underlies social action. Culture in the wide sense is continuously being shaped by culture in the narrower senses of the arts and ethics, the everyday forms of artistic expression from cuisine, to music, to fashion, to film, to interior design, and the prevailing views of morality. In Chapters 5 and 6, we address the artifacts of popular culture and culture as morality, but these are understood in relation to this larger sense of culture as a framework of meaning.

When "culture as art" is taken up, "elite" or "high" culture is in part, but not primarily, what is meant. In the visual arts, cultural studies does not just study nineteenth-century painting but interprets graffiti and rock album covers. In drama it studies Shakespearean plays but also television situation comedies. In literature it studies not only sonnets but romance novels and science fiction. In music, it takes up not only Beethoven's string quartets but also rap and hip hop. In dance, it looks at not only ballet but street theater and music video choreography. In "multimedia" it studies Italian opera and also interactive hypertext CD ROM novels. Under "culture" we include popular culture, from films to magazine advertisements, from bumper stickers to poetry slams. These images are important because on the one hand, they are reflections of a changing environment, and on the other, they help to shape the way we make decisions. In short, they are the way we interpret our world.

Cultural studies is not only widening the scope of the cultural artifacts it studies, it is exploring new ways of seeing artifacts. It resists the strong tendency to treat culture as an object, as a static, unchanging thing, or as a homogeneous unity. It struggles to be radically self-reflective, asking about the researcher's own relationship to the cultural phenomena under study. By contrast, social scientists in general, and economists especially, have tended to treat culture (when they refer to it at all) as an object, as an external thing to be measured. To draw statistically significant answers they go for less immersion in the details of any one case, and for more cases.

The case of economic development, which might seem to be a matter of material, measurable phenomena, is a good example of the pervasive importance of culture. To be sure, if we want to determine the wealth-generating potential of a society we do need to ask about some readily observable factors, such as its mineral resources, access to the sea, climate, yearly rainfall, and other factors that may lend themselves to useful quantitative analysis. When we get around to more inherently subjective factors, however, such as the *value* of the society's stock of capital, the *quality* of its legal and monetary institutions, or of its prevailing regulatory policies, more qualitative, interpretive work is needed.

The most quantitative study is measuring *something*, and the nature of the things being counted must either be assumed to be already known, or needs to be explained. The most "objective" factors are always interpreted, though of course we may find that not much discussion is needed about some matters. Extensive interviewing about what the recorder meant by "inch" is not normally necessary to get the annual rainfall right. But when we are talking about issues like evaluating a society's capital stock, or its regulatory policy, or its potential for entrepreneurial development, we do need to know – close-up – the agents' own interpretations of the phenomena. We need to get access to what many scholars would call the culture. To get the research off the ground, or perhaps we should say, to get its feet *on* the ground, we need the kind of intimacy with the "subjective" details that we can call ethnographic contact. (A fascinating example of the insight into human affairs that is afforded by close-up ethnographic contact is the book *A History of Private Life* edited by Paul Veyne 1987.) There is a cultural meaning underlying all human action, but some questions, such as a society's entrepreneurial growth potential, are not like measuring rainfall. They require extensive ethnographic contact to be understood.

In an overview of the cultural studies literature, Simon During (1993a: 21) observes that "For cultural studies, knowledge based on statistical techniques belongs to the processes which 'normalize' society and stand in opposition to cultural studies' respect for the marginal subject." To us this does not quite add up to any kind of principled rejection of the use of statistics, but there may well be good reasons here to focus more on case studies. This sort of subject matter does seem to lend itself to the "getting up close" approach, striving for ethnographic contact, rather than the "stepping back" approach, striving for statistical regularity. The focus on the "marginal subject," for example, can help us to appreciate the role of the entrepreneur who sees things differently from conventional thinking. The cultural regularities reported in most statistical scholarship do not seem to tell us much we did not think we knew already. By contrast close-up historical and ethnographic studies of culture seem packed with interesting details. In practice the loss in breadth seems more than made up for by the gain in depth.

But cultural studies also enriches traditional ethnography with a sophisticated appreciation, drawn from the fields of philosophy and literary theory, of the nature of the efforts of understanding that are under way. Understanding is likened to the reading of a text, only the word "text" comes to signify anything that is open to interpretation (see Ricoeur 1971). The process of interpretation is a "polysemic" one, that is, one in which a variety of radically diverse readings are possible. When the alternative voices of this dialogue are able to come to an understanding of one another, this can be the source of a creative process for the production of new meaning. It is not a process that is unidirectionally dictated by either the text or the reader, but an on-going interplay, a mediation among perspectives. It is the sort of process Friedrich Hayek labels a "spontaneous order" (see Hayek 1948; Lavoie 1990c, 1990d).

The view that a society's culture, unlike its policies or institutions, is given, and fixed, or nearly impossible to change, is what sociologist Peter Berger, a keen observer of cultural aspects of economic performance, calls the "Ancient Curse" theory of culture. Cultural studies shows that culture is not an immutable given with which a society must learn to live. Nor is it homogenous within nations, or even within families. It is a complex of diverse tensions, ever evolving, always open to new manifestations and permutations.

What the Ancient Curse approach to culture obscures is the very essence of culture: the fact that it is not a static thing but an ongoing process. Culture is not the dead hand of the past constraining our actions to traditions as contrasted with our Reason. It is the very site of our reasoning activities, shaping what we find persuasive, and being shaped by our participation in dialogue. It is not a single, unified thing but a complex of conflicting tensions and proclivities. It is the locus of, and the framework that gives meaning to, our efforts to change ourselves and our societies.

We may be more accustomed to thinking of the arts as a process, and it is widely understood that we need to grant artists freedoms in order to allow the artistic sphere of our lives to flourish. Artistic change takes place through a discursive process where the individual artist offers an alternative interpretation of something. In turn, another artist may challenge this view with a different interpretation. Religion is also seen as an ongoing conversation which has its basis in culture. What is perhaps less obvious is that culture also allows for the "dialogue" of the scientific and political spheres of our lives to take place.

And what is rarely appreciated is that culture is what underlies the dialogue of the market, as well. Culture provides the framework of values, a shared language if you will, which allows us to participate in these conversations. Before the rise of cultural studies, analyses of commercial culture often assumed a unidirectional process whereby consumers were being manipulated by advertising into buying the commodities produced by capitalist firms. Critical theorists had tended to treat the consumer as a helpless victim. Contemporary cultural studies research shows that the relationship between the producers and consumers is more complex. One of the leading contributors to the cultural studies literature, Stuart Hall (1980: 90–103), talks in terms of an encoding and decoding process, that is, the specific manner in which cultural artifacts undergo an interpretive process through which their meaning and significance is produced or encoded and then consumed or decoded. He appreciates the multiplicity of decodings the consumer or "spectator" can have in response to the market's outlay of commodities. Habermas ([1962] 1989), in his 1962 book on the changes mass media and the science of public opinion management have on our culture, was still treating the process in a unidirectional way. Later he comments (Habermas 1992a: 439) on the way Hall's approach influenced his thinking about the changes mass media have had on culture:

> Stuart Hall's distinction between three different interpretive strategies on the part of spectators (who either submit to the structure of what is being offered, take an oppositional stance, or synthesize it with their own interpretations) illustrates well how the perspective has changed from the older explanatory models still assuming linear causal processes.

When the cultural studies scholar examines a culture, an active reading is being undertaken of a "text" and the text is inherently open to a number of different interpretations. Moreover, the "text" being read, the culture being examined, is itself a process of mutual reading and rereading by its participants, of other "texts," that is, meaningful actions and artifacts of other persons. Getting a better understanding of how all this "reading" takes place helps us to see how culture shapes economic processes. We can expand the metaphor of "the text" to market processes. A market is not so much a physical, objective thing, it is more like a text which is open to several possible "readings." Economic entrepreneurship can in this sense be seen as an ability to read the market text.

2.2   Culture and economy in the modernist epoch

When assessing the economy of a country, professional economists study inflation, unemployment, growth rates, leading indicators, and regulatory policy. Far less often in assessing our economic prospects do we direct our attention to the cultural fabric (see, for example, Polly Hill's *Development Economics on Trial* 1986). When looking into business decision-making, economists direct attention to a careful analysis of the monetary costs and benefits, but rarely suggest that issues of moral responsibility within corporate culture may also be involved. Cultural studies scholars would be inclined to ask: "What is it about *our* culture, the culture of professional economists, that shapes what we pay attention to, and what we ignore?" This section suggests that the prevailing philosophical attitudes of our time are responsible for the neglect economists have paid to culture. Thus here we ask what is wrong with economics that leaves it so silent on so important a topic, while the next chapter asks what is right with economics, how much of what it does say can be integrated with and enhance what cultural studies is doing.

This study argues that culture lies at the foundation both of market and political processes. By examining cultural attitudes which influence these processes, we are in a better position to identify elements which are detrimental as well as those which are beneficial to what we think of as economic and political progress. Social institutions work to protect and improve our democratic political values, and work to improve our standards of living, to the extent they ever do work, only because there is a set of loosely shared values, which provides for the acceptance of the norms that sustain those institutions. A legal system cannot provide the rule of law if there is no generally accepted attitude about justice. A property rights system will not allow for the expansion of trade if there is no commonly accepted notion of ownership. The presence of a written Constitution will be of little help if the underlying cultural norms which maintain its legitimacy are dead. If the cultural norms which have fostered these vital institutions are eroded away, we may no longer be able to rely upon the benefits which they have traditionally conveyed, to varying degrees, upon societies.

The social sciences have been kept from adequately coping with culture as a result of the domination of what we have been calling its "modernistic" philosophical presuppositions, which have been especially limiting in the field of economics. Modernism distorts economics, preventing it from becoming the culturally relevant discipline it could be, and the modernist training of economists tends to leave them poorly equipped for the study of culture. The biases modernism imparts to economics, which we will label formalism, quantitativism, and causalism, are each in their own way keeping the field from getting a handle on culture.

Formalism can be defined as getting so caught up in the pyrotechnical difficulties of one's theory that one loses sight altogether of the practical problems it was invented to solve. In economics, formalism takes the form of an infatuation with mathematical technique. If you ever pick up contemporary journals of economics you get the point. There are many wonderful questions that have been posed throughout the history of economics which are being ignored because such a premium is put on technical theory-building of the kind that puts theory far away from the "life-world," the world of everyday existence. Cultural studies does not suffer from the particular kind of formalism, a bias for mathematical and statistical modes of discourse, that is prevalent in economics. After all it arises mainly from literature departments, and has no particular guilt complex about expressing its meaning in words. But to be fair we have to admit that some of the cultural studies literature succumbs to its own kinds of formalism in its excessive construction of theoretical jargon and overcomplicated conceptual apparati. So, all we mean by formalism is something that distances the theory from real-world problems, where that distancing can happen in a variety of ways.

Modernism also brings about a narrowing of economists' attitudes toward the nature of empirical work, which might be called *"quantitativism."* Empirical research in economics today is, in the minds of many economists, synonymous with econometrics. Sophisticated statistics tends to crowd out both more simple and straightforward uses of statistics, and non-statistical, qualitative empirical investigations. Now of course, unlike a great deal of mathematical theorizing, statistical economics does at least have some practical usefulness, that is, you can do quantitative studies of real-world questions, and can try to discern meaningful patterns in the numbers. But in contemporary economic empirical work there is a tendency to ask *only* the kind of questions to which sophisticated econometric tools can be applied. In some journals the only questions asked are quantitative, so that the first condition of a respectable empirical study is making sure you have a large enough sample size to be able to draw statistically generalizable conclusions from it.

But there is another whole kind of empirical work that is highly regarded outside of economics, ethnography and archival-historical research, which involves very close-up studies of the complex details in their specific contexts. Here the rich description and interpretation of the context is what is important, and the size of the sample is necessarily (for economic reasons) small. Earlier we stated that empirical research is, "in the minds of many economists," synonymous with econometrics. But on the margins of all the econometrics, can be found a mini-industry of more interpretive and more interdisciplinary modes of empirical economic research (see for example the research that is conducted at such journals as *Business History Review*, the *Journal of Economic History, Economic History Review, Research in Economic History, Explorations in Entrepreneurial History,* the *Journal of Development Economics,* the *Journal of European Economic History,* or the *Scandinavian Economic History Review*).

Sometimes down-to-earth, close-up, archival research does not just sit at the margins but makes a major impact on economists' thinking, such as when Ronald Coase did his empirical study of the supply of lighthouse services (1974) and of the origins of the legal allocation of property rights in the electromagnetic spectrum (1959). Ethnography and archival history (we will call it ethnography for short) are essentially what anthropologists are doing when they study a traditional society, what management scholars do when they apply the case study method, what business historians do when they study the history of firms, and what economic historians and even historians of economic thought are really doing.

And this is, in our view, how you get at culture. It is by way of intimate, detailed, qualitative research, immersed in the complex context of *one* particular situation, that you can begin to get a handle on culture. This immersion in a single case makes for excellent ethnography, but as economists tend to look at it, a sample size of one makes for lousy statistical inference. As a result, there is a whole way of getting access to the real world which is denied to most economists, and this way of knowing happens to be the one which is best suited to studying culture. (Examples to us of useful work in economic ethnography are Clark 1994; Ensminger 1992; Hill 1963; Robben 1989; and Robertson 1984.)

Ethnography is itself a difficult empirical method which requires quite a different sort of training from the kind that graduate schools of economics supply, so economists are usually not predisposed to try this sort of thing. Clearly, if you cannot study culture you cannot study how it applies to entrepreneurship and economic development. We think if you cannot do ethnography, you cannot study culture.

If you could get an economist to disregard these methodological obstacles to the study of culture, there would still remain another problem: *causalism.* Many economists are stuck on the idea of measuring mechanistic causation. To many economists, explanations that are not fully mechanistic are necessarily unintelligible (see for example the revealing comments by Robert Lucas and others in Arjo Klamer's book, *Conversations with Economists* 1983). The way economists would be inclined to pose the question of the role of culture in economic growth is that they would ask whether "cultural factors" are a (statistically) significant cause of growth. They might, for example, try comparing political factors with cultural factors, to see which tend to dominate. Is it more important for growth that there be favorable political factors, such as low marginal tax rates, or that there be favorable cultural factors, such as a high regard for frugality?

Without denying the value of these questions, cultural studies has other, we think more fundamental, questions in mind. The problem with only looking at culture as a specific causal factor is that it underestimates the pervasiveness of culture in all social causes. As we have argued, culture is an *aspect* of political, economic, psychological, and sociological causal factors, rather than another distinct cause alongside these factors. It is the level of meaning underneath social action, so that to compare it with a particular causal factor, such as political conditions, is to fail to comprehend its larger significance. Low marginal tax rates are themselves shaped by cultural meanings, and the way they affect action depends on cultural interpretations. Indeed it is difficult to identify specific factors which are distinguishable from others by being "cultural." The anthropologist Clifford Geertz (1973: 50–1) makes this point eloquently.

> Our ideas, our values, our acts, even our emotions, are ... cultural products – products manufactured, indeed, out of tendencies, capacities, and dispositions with which we were born, but manufactured nonetheless. Chartres is made of stone and glass. But not just stone and glass; it is a cathedral, and not only a cathedral, but a particular cathedral built at a particular time by certain members of a particular society. To understand what it means, to perceive it for what it is, you need to know rather more than the generic properties of stone and glass and rather more than what is common to all cathedrals. You need to understand also – and, in my opinion, most critically – the specific concepts of the relations among God, man, and architecture that, since they have governed its creation, it consequently embodies. It is no different with men: they, too, every last one of them, are cultural artifacts.

Culture is everywhere, so for economists and other social scientists intent on doing comparative causal analysis, it is nowhere. How can one say how important it is if it cannot be isolated as a distinct factor?

To sum up, culture is the underlying context that makes the world meaningful, that gives any particular cause meaning. The useful question to ask is not one that tries to gauge the extent to which culture, as opposed to, say, incentives, shapes behavior. Culture is best seen as an aspect of all the factors of social influence. Culture is the domain of shared and conflicting meanings, and it is these meanings which make incentives, political possibilities, entrepreneurial opportunities, and other "causal factors" what they are. It does not stand as a separate cause of changes; it constitutes the meaning of the factors which do cause the changes. (See Gudeman 1986 for an interesting discussion of the primary metaphors at work in different economic contexts and the way this shapes the way the economic processes work.)

And yet in questioning mechanical causation, we are not asking that we abandon the explanatory aspirations of the social sciences. While critical of objectivistic causal explanations, the analysis of cultural processes can still offer a coherent narrative account of how events unfold. The shift from the sort of literary criticism that was focussed on disembodied literary works, presumed to be cut off from their social context, to the study of the cultural dynamics that are going on in real life, is precisely what the emerging field of cultural studies is all about. In the narratives by which we give historical accounts of how social change occurs, or how a business enterprise gets built, can be found a form of "causal explanation" that is more appropriate to its subject matter than the mechanistic forms of explanation that continue to limit the social sciences.

Although in this sense it can be misleading to talk of "cultural factors" we can legitimately ask about the specific ways in which cultural meanings shape the institutions and practices of societies. The difficulty here is methodological: many social scientists only know how to ask statistical explanatory questions, and do not know how to engage in interpretive ethnographic inquiry, how to construct coherent historical narratives, how to mine the archives for historical clues, how to interview the participants to economic processes, how to grapple with the ethical ambiguities of business decisions. This is where they have the most to learn from the field of cultural studies. Most of the other social sciences have already enjoyed a major reaction against modernist presuppositions in the form of what has been called "interpretive" social science. In the case of economics, such a reaction is barely beginning.

2.3   The evolution of the field of cultural studies

Accounts of the rise of the distinct field that is now called "cultural studies" often refer back to the work of a handful of British literary theorists in the late 1950s, especially Richard Hoggart, who founded the Birmingham Centre for Contemporary Cultural Studies (CCCS), and Raymond Williams. The CCCS, whose works have fundamentally shaped the field, fueled a new convergence between literature, ethnography, and continental philosophy that has come to be called cultural studies. The field arose on behalf of a certain approach to the study of the meaning of contemporary everyday life, an approach that is highly philosophical in its theorizing, and ethnographic in its empirical work.

This was also a field that was born with a distinctly and forthrightly "leftist" ideological orientation. The movement some have called "cultural Marxism" caught on with the rise of the New Left in Britain, in the late 1960s, and its early years echoed all the controversies within European Marxism. One scholar (Pinkney 1991: 584) describes Williams as "a founder of the British 'New Left', editing its *May Day Manifesto* in 1967." Hoggart's *The Uses of Literacy* (1957) is a celebration of those elements of working-class culture that are still untainted with commercialism, combined with a Marxist critique of modern, mass culture. Many contemporary cultural studies scholars have come to see this as a "schizo-phrenic" attitude (During 1993a: 3) trying to embrace the popular while condemning markets. But cultural studies has never rejected its original theme: that students of culture need to go out into the field and get some ethnographic contact with the living culture of ordinary folks.

In style many scholars in the field continue to exude the radical left, and often speak in solemn tones about the workings of "late capitalism"; however, important shifts have taken place in the substance of its arguments that move it away from the traditional left's attitudes toward markets and government policy. The substantive shifts the field has undergone – a turn away from a certain literary formalism and elitism that had distanced it from commercial culture – may well come to mark a profound change in the whole meaning of "the left." Market transactions used automatically to imply crass commercialism and the intrusion of corporate power into the everyday lives of ordinary people. To many cultural studies scholars today, ordinary people are understood to be genuine and influential participants in markets, and the commercial cultural products they buy and sell are often taken to be deserving of our deepest respect.

Cultural studies is essentially a response to the mainstream views of literary theory in the 1950s and 1960s, prominent among which are the so-called New Criticism and the Frankfurt School. One could call the Frankfurt School the field's "left wing" but even the "conservative wing," the New Criticism, has a tradition of deep distrust for markets. Ideologically the New Criticism tended to consider cultural products which were successful in the market to be *for that very reason* suspect. The job of the literary critic was to illuminate the superiority of High Culture over the lowly pseudo-culture of the masses.

The New Critics always looked for the essential unitary meaning of the text, often in terms of some sort of ironic theme it was conveying, and tended to remain blind to internal fragmentations and incoherencies. It took this singular meaning of the text to be fixed and permanent, not fleeting and dependent on the reader's context. Contemporary cultural studies in contrast, sees texts as fragmented and open to multiple readings, and to an evolution of ever-new readings through time.

New Critical literary theory also suffered from a form of formalism, which has kept it from confronting practical issues, such as the cultural sources of economic prosperity. Just as economics has been separating itself from reality by its mathematical formalism, so literary criticism, especially in the heyday of the "New Criticism," had been separating itself from reality by its own brand of formalism. In New Criticism, the main idea was to look at texts such as a great poem from John Donne or a Shakespeare sonnet, and to concentrate on how to interpret that text, draw out subtle meanings from it, and analyze it exclusively apart from the rest of the world, to which it is admitted to be in fact connected. In the New Criticism there is a deliberate attempt to argue that you are not being a good literary critic if you try to say that Shakespeare somehow relates to his time, that knowing something about English politics, or social mores, or economic circumstances, of the day might be of some importance in understanding King Lear. That would be to politicize it, or sociologize it, or economize it, or in other words to take it out of the English

Department. It is as if they were saying, "To make it *our* field we have got to make sure it is only literary critical tools that are put to work on this text."

The Frankfurt School approach, for its part, had the deepest disdain for the cultural orientation of the general public. It "explained" why the masses did not appreciate True Art by showing how capitalism leads people into a "false consciousness." Thus at one point it attempted to explain why people liked jazz and not the latest developments in twelve-tone music; and then when jazz became highbrow, it explained why the masses listen to rock and roll. The Frankfurt School and other Marxist approaches to literature never bought into the New Critics' assumption that literary texts were above and severed from the everyday world, that is, from commercial markets, but for them the relationship between art and the market was a strictly antagonistic one. Markets represented a negative force that was systematically eroding culture.

Both for conservative New Critics and radical Frankfurt Schoolers, for something to be commercially successful in the market was tantamount for it to disqualify itself as genuine culture. As Barbara Herrnstein Smith (1988: 26) points out:

> ... [T]he revulsion of academics and intellectuals at the actual literary preferences, forms of aesthetic enjoyment, and general modes of cultural consumption of nonacademics and nonintellectuals – including those whose political emancipation they may otherwise seek to promote – has been a familiar feature of the cultural-political scene since at least the 1930s. It will not do, of course, simply to label this "snobbery" or "elitism," for it is the product of multiple and quite complexly related psychological, sociological, and ideological elements which, moreover, are played out differently under different historical, social, and institutional conditions and therefore require very careful analysis. It is clear, however, that the oppositional cultural theory and conservative humanism have repeatedly generated strictly parallel (and indeed, often indistinguishable) accounts to explain the tastes of other people in such a way as to justify the academic intellectual's revulsion at them.

What was unavailable within literary theory until fairly recently was an account of the relationship between markets and culture that sees them as (at least potentially) mutually supportive. This is what contemporary work on popular culture within the cultural studies field is beginning to create.

At its birth, the new interdisciplinary field of cultural studies was still more confident than it should have been of the leftist biases against markets that it inherited from its predecessors in English, Anthropology, Sociology, Art, History, and Philosophy departments. Its founders such as Hoggart and Williams celebrated popular art in the sense of the folklore of the working class, but were still trying to indict all of commercial culture as an intrusion by capitalism into the properly non-commercialized realm of art. But already there was something importantly different here from the previous literature on culture. Raymond Williams was honing in on an understanding of the pervasiveness of cultural process in all of social life, and was explicitly challenging the orthodox Marxist privileging of the "base" (or material conditions) over the "superstructure" (a category which includes all cultural influences). Ideas and values matter, and are not merely symptoms of material circumstances. And the ideas and values that matter *especially* are those that are so fundamental to a person's thinking that they are hidden from view, that is, those that are built into the culture.

The first decade or so of cultural studies research was firmly within the tradition of Hoggart's and Williams' early work. The everyday folks being studied, Simon During (1993a: 10) says, "are primarily viewed as being engaged in symbolic struggle with the larger social system," and are not seen as sometimes simply "trying to have fun or to construct a mode of life for themselves." What begins to happen in the evolution of cultural studies is that the everyday folks being so respectfully studied in the field actually get listened to. Cultural studies came to see the reading of culture as a hermeneutical or interpretive problem, a problem of translation or mediation between divergent world-views. It became self-conscious about the fact that academics occupy a somewhat sheltered culture of their own, so it struggled to avoid forcing its own categories onto the subjects under study. And as a result it has come increasingly to respect the more market-friendly values of the ordinary people. The "masses" stop getting treated as helpless victims of commercialization who are to be pitied for having been denied the high culture we academics enjoy, and start being treated as active and creative contributors to culture.

This can be described as happening in two stages. First it took a theoretical turn, as cultural studies scholars made more complex and interesting their conception of the way ordinary people consume culture. In the 1970s cultural studies fell under the influence of French theories, at first, Marxist structuralism, especially the work of Louis Althusser, but then a variety of non-Marxist theorists, including Michel Foucault (1972) and Pierre Bourdieu (1984). French theory expanded the conceptual apparati of culture studies beyond both the cultural nationalism (see Section 4.1.2 on page 59) of the New Critics and the orthodox Marxist class analysis of the Frankfurt School. It led to a "more fragmented" analysis by introducing notions such as Bourdieu's (1993) idea of "social fields," that can denote families, workplaces, educational institutions, political parties, etc., each of which, as During (1993a: 11) puts it, "contains its own 'imaginary,' its own promise and image of satisfaction and success, its own possibilities for pleasure." (See also Douglas and Isherwood 1979.)

In their field work cultural studies scholars found their subjects not just succumbing to cultural hegemonies they did not want to belong to, but creatively "reading" the culture in their own ways and actively choosing "social fields" to belong to. Even for the most marginalized subcultural groups who see little of the dominant culture as their own, possibilities exist, as During (1993a: 11) says, "for 'transgressive undermining' or 'festive' overturning of routines and hierarchies through passive resistance, ironical mimicry, symbolic inversion, orgiastic letting go, even day-dreaming ..." The process of cultural reception – the way consumers read the meaning of cultural products – comes to be understood as a complex interaction, in which consumers are not only manipulated by the culture industry, but always have some recourse to respond in their own fashion, to appropriate meanings in their own ways.

During (1993a: 12–13) describes the significance of this "second phase" of cultural studies:

> The French model breaks away from earlier forms of cultural studies. ... [I]t cannot affirm a central agency that might direct a number of fields to provide a more equitable distribution of resources. In this it is remote from traditional social democratic politics. Instead there is a drift to affirm both culture's Utopian force and those forms of resistance ... only possible in the cracks and gaps of the larger ... system.

Cultural studies was at this time reacting to the cultural conservatism that accompanied the rise of the Thatcherite movement. As During (1993a: 13) notes: "it was in the context of the new right's emergence that ... after absorbing French theory, the discipline oriented itself toward what Cornel West ... calls the 'culture of difference' and became a genuinely global movement." The focus of attention was shifting away from trying to influence the centralized "social democratic power bloc," and instead trying to engage with everyday people "on the ground." The people being studied in fact did not see themselves primarily in terms of the National Culture (New Criticism) or in terms of resistance or acquiescence to Capital (Frankfurt School), but seem to have developed their own social fields. Students of culture who

> identified themselves as feminists, members of a particular ethnic or sexual preference group rather than of a class or a nation, say, were interested in studying culture and theory on their own terms, and were ready for more fragmented models of culture and society – models which, strangely enough, echoed Mrs. Thatcher's famous and radical apothegm: "There is no such thing as '*society*'." (During 1993a: 16)

Stage Two Cultural Studies, in other words, stops letting "culture" stand in for the concepts of nation or the state, but decisively moves toward the study of cultures themselves, in all their fascinating fragmentation and diversity. Stage Three, During (1993a: 17) says, is when the field "began to celebrate commercial culture" as an important social field in itself. Make no mistake, "leftist" views are still prevalent among these academics. There is definite hesitation about taking this step, and many apologies are made for what may appear to be concessions to capitalism. But in the end the "cultural populism" movement is taking this step. It already constitutes an important change in the whole way the left is thinking about commercial life, a change that is noted by During (1993a: 16):

> [T]he affirmation of otherness and difference ... belong[s] to a looser, more pluralistic and post-modern, conceptual model than those which insist that capitalism and the free market produce interests that are *structurally* unequal and in conflict with each other. Unlike social democratic thought, the new cultural studies no longer aimed at a radical transfiguration of the whole system of social fields.

The new field of cultural studies would now begin shedding much of the old leftist agenda and start taking seriously the task of trying to understand a culture. Against the formalism of New Criticism, there has been a powerful return to the notion that one can best understand cultural artifacts not by putting them on theoretical pedestals, but by placing them in their specific historical contexts. Against the Frankfurt School's and New Critics' academic sneering at commercial culture has arisen the powerful cultural populism movement that takes seriously what everyday people enjoy as art. Indeed today the overwhelming force of the most highly regarded work in the cultural studies field is a rebellion against exactly these elitist and formalist attitudes.

New Critical formalism has been so thoroughly routed that there is at least as much likelihood of getting the present mainstream of cultural studies researchers to engage in a meaningful confrontation with real-world problems of market institutions as there is of getting the mainstream of the economics profession, which is still too deeply mired in its formalism, to do so. While there is no clear successor school to the New Critics, all of the so-called post-structuralist schools, from Deconstruction to Semiotics, from Hermeneutics to Foucaultian Genealogy, agree that the study of culture needs to connect to social contexts. The formalistic idea of studying texts in themselves, dwelling on their internal structure alone, is dead.

The Frankfurt School of Critical Theory, meanwhile, has been undergoing significant transformations at the hands of such social theorists as Habermas, Karl-Otto Apel, Claus Offe, and Albrecht Wellmer. Critical Theorists today are as likely to express skepticism about the New Class of bureaucratic power-wielders as they are to express distrust of business corporations. Political attention is turning away from statist solutions imposed from above, and toward an exploration of the "public sphere," the realm of public discourse about our mutual rights and responsibilities.

Habermas (1992a: 443) insists, contrary to orthodox Marxism, that, as Thatcher says, there is no such thing as "society." He points out that "the presumption that society as a whole can be conceived as an association writ large, directing itself via the media of law and political power, has become entirely implausible in view of the high level of complexity of functionally differentiated societies." The left needs to learn from the errors of traditional Marxism.

> The bankruptcy of state socialism now witnessed has once again confirmed that a modern, market-regulated economic system cannot be switched as one pleases, from a monetary mechanism to one involving administrative power and democratic decision making, without threatening its performance capacity. Additionally, our experiences with a social-welfare state being pushed to its limits have sensitized us to the phenomena of bureaucratization and intrusive legalism ... These pathological effects are consequences of the state's interventions in spheres of activity structured in a manner that renders the legal-administrative mode of regulating them inappropriate. (1992a: 436)

Habermas, to be sure, still wants to treat markets as a "System" external, and potentially threatening, to culture, not as an integral part of it. He seems to want to conceive of public discourse as ideally taking place outside not only of government but of *any* real institutional context, in some kind of "ideal speech community," which is devoid of markets. But this position has been specifically challenged by writers who call for a notion of public discourse that is more oriented to actual people in real institutions (see for example Walzer 1990; Warnke 1990a, 1990b), so that this conversation is ripe for a more integrative analysis of markets. Critical theory today is an utterly different thing from the old days of the Frankfurt School Marxists. Among some of these writers there is no more of the facile condemnations of markets there used to be, but instead a willingness to accept the view that markets can be a truly progressive force.

2.4   Shifting the site of "politics"

The scholarship of contemporary Critical Theory represents a significant opportunity to help us move beyond the traditional left/right spectrum. Habermas and others (see McCarthy 1992; Benhabib 1992; Benhabib and Dallmayr 1990; Taylor 1990) are working to develop an understanding of the nature of civil society, of the public sphere, of political culture, which profoundly shifts the ground of public policy thinking away from the habit the left had fallen into of turning over all its aspirations to the state. Many on the left are coming to realize that the changes in society they hope for can best be achieved in the "politics" of day-to-day life, in the way we conduct ourselves with others on the job, in schools, at home, in our local communities. The governmental politics the left used to believe in is proving itself inadequate to the democratic tasks we have set it. Many are seeing that, as Hannah Arendt (1958, 1968) argued, in order to develop, cultivate and protect a public sphere that would be adequate to our implicit notions of democracy, it is necessary to protect the private sphere from intrusions by the state. (For an excellent analysis of Arendt's contribution to the idea of the political, see Villa 1996.)

Advocates of the traditional classical liberal and libertarian approach to rights have long argued that respect for one another's *rights* is necessary for a free society, but some have claimed that respect for each other's *values*, an openness to one another's differences, is a fundamentally different matter, and is unnecessary. It is certainly true that a free society is not dependent upon an uncritical acceptance of *all* values. In fact, we would say that a free society means that many values will be rejected, for example, some religious values that suggest that women are the property of their husbands or fathers. But some libertarians miss an important point – a point which critical theorists such as Habermas, Wellmer, and Benhabib elaborate eloquently – when they suggest that all we have to do is respect each other's rights and that we do not have to respect *anybody* else's values. They argue as if rights operate outside of the cultural realm, outside of the dialogue regarding values.

Those cultural studies scholars who are focusing on the importance of individual rights are reminding us of the cultural context from which a strong belief in rights first emerged. Where do our rights regarding individual expression and religious freedom come from? In our context, anyway, they have emerged out of a dialogue concerning religious tolerance, the role of the state, etc. The discussion of values has informed the historical treatment of rights from the beginning (see Richard Ashcraft 1986: 106–27).

Thus, we cannot separate the issues of "respecting divergent values" and "respecting each other's rights" as easily as liberal theory often suggests. Civil society cannot only rest upon respecting each other's rights without also some measure of openness towards the values of others. First, many of the conflicts we face in the realm of values are not so easily resolved through a reliance upon rights. The abortion issue is an obvious example. To say that a discussion of rights will resolve all these problems is to diminish the significance of the cultural cleavages that have developed. Further the only way to resolve such conflicts is to engage in open discourse – to attempt to engage in mutual understanding. Such a dialogue can only take place if a range of values is respected, if not adopted. In short, civil society depends upon a genuine openness and respect for the "other." Again, this is not to suggest that values should be accepted uncritically, rather, that a multitude of values will have to exist – by definition – in any dialogue regarding values.

Indeed, we are deploying a very specific notion of openness here, one which has been developed in the hermeneutics literature. We do not consider such openness to amount to disinterestedness, or some sort of flabby relativism in which all points of view are uncritically accepted as equally valid, or to be some sort of abstract ideal that is only realizable to disembodied souls in institutional vacuums. To be open to another point of view means to be able to take its truth-claims seriously, to dare to risk one's own point of view against the point of view of the other. A tolerance based on value-freedom and detachment, or on relativism, or on the Habermasian notion of an ideal speech community, might lead to a position whereby extreme challenges to prevailing orthodoxy are excluded as "unreasonable," as disturbances of the discursive peace, so to speak. But hermeneutical openness insists that divergent voices really be *listened* to, even where they constitute a challenge that is extraordinarily disturbing. Not only polite and tame contributions to existing discussions, but also uncompromising challenges to prevailing views, for example, those of the abolitionist movement in nineteenth-century America, are, from this point of view, part of what is meant by open discourse.

This notion of openness to others is arguably the core political value of a free society, a common value behind both a free market economy, which thrives on the openness of exchange, and a democratic polity, which thrives on the openness of public discourse (see Lavoie 1992, 1993, 1995). In the writings of several contributors to the cultural studies literature the very idea of democracy is being reconceived as not primarily an issue about government or voting, but as an issue about culture, about the manner in which we talk and otherwise engage with one another. As the left turns from a naive faith in government, and tries to rethink the idea of democracy in a non-coercive way, the whole ideological landscape is shifting. Critical theorist Seyla Benhabib (1992: 94) points out how feminist scholarship needs to change in this regard:

> When ... issues like child rearing; care for the sick, the young, and the elderly; reproductive freedoms; domestic violence; child abuse; and the constitution of sexual identities go public in our societies, more often than not a "patriarchal-capitalist-disciplinary bureaucracy" has resulted. These bureaucracies have frequently disempowered women and have set the agenda for public debate and participation. ... A critical model of public space is necessary to enable us to draw the line between "juridification" ... on the one hand and making public, in the sense of making accessible to debate, reflection, action, and moral-political transformation, on the other. To make issues of common concern public in this second sense means making them increasingly accessible to discursive will formation; it means to democratize them; it means bringing them under standards of moral reflection compatible with autonomous, postconventional identities. As feminists, we have lacked a critical model that can distinguish between the bureaucratic administration of needs and collective democratic empowerment over them.

The struggle for recognition takes place in office politics and within family life, where women or minorities or those with unorthodox lifestyles strive to attain the status of genuine citizens in civil society.

The cultural conservatives can see only the old left here. In gender studies or studies of the gay community, or of the Harlem ghetto they can see only a "politicization" of the private sphere, the intrusion of government into more of our lives. Indeed, interventionist government solutions often have been sought to right old wrongs, for example by mandating more welfare spending. But government failure has not been recognized only by those on the political right. By seeking to understand the welfare system from the perspective of the recipients themselves, many within cultural studies have also come to appreciate the insidious cycle of dependence to which the state subjects its poorest citizens. Many within cultural studies are turning away from governmental and legal policies as the panacea, and are calling for respectful treatment in everyday life of those who have been powerless.

Take, for example, the book by Pearl and Samuel Oliner called *Toward a Caring Society* (1995: 1–2), which opens by emphasizing how different their thesis is from a book with a similar title by Irving Bernstein (1985).

> The "caring society" Bernstein describes was the government's creation: it was the welfare state the New Deal under Franklin Delano Roosevelt designed to address unemployment through such measures as unemployment relief, welfare programs, the protection of the right of workers to organize and bargain collectively, and old age pensions.
>
> ... But as we see it, no government can resolve today's non-care problems, nor can any political program or structural change eliminate them, although they can help facilitate solutions. Change, we believe, needs to come primarily from the "inside out" – that is, from individuals finding, nurturing, and creating the conditions that promote care within the social institutions in which they routinely live their lives.

In a sense what cultural studies is doing is shifting the *site* of politics, even of our whole notion of "public policy," away from what has been the left's preoccupation with the state, and toward the "politics" of everyday life. Politics is not to be seen merely as the special interest politics and lobbying, the vote mongering and public opinion manipulation we associate with professional politicians. Instead the idea of "the political" can be seen, as Hannah Arendt discussed it, as a matter of changing society from the inside out.

Classical liberal and libertarian writers, due to their urgent sense that the particular form of government-centered politics that has marked our time is a dangerous threat to liberty, have historically underemphasized the legitimate and necessary sense of "the political" in our lives. Moreover, because of the strong influence of reductionistic economic thinking in both right-wing and left-wing political thought, there has been a tendency to reduce political action to what Arendt called "fabrication," to the model of the isolated man gaining mastery over nature. But it is not enough to enjoy negative freedom, to be free as isolated individuals from interference by others. We have a need to be free in the positive sense, of having an ability to initiate action in society with our fellow citizens. Arendt emphasizes the social aspects in her concept of "action."

> Action, as distinguished from fabrication, is never possible in isolation; to be isolated is to be deprived of the capacity to act. Action and speech need the surrounding presence of others no less than fabrication needs the surrounding presence of nature for its material, and of a world in which to place the finished product. ... The popular belief in a "strong man" who, isolated against others, owes his strength to his being alone is either sheer superstition, based on the delusion that we can "make" something in the realm of human affairs – "make" institutions or laws, for instance, as we make tables and chairs, or make men "better" or "worse" – or it is conscious despair of all action, political and non-political, coupled with the utopian hope that it may be possible to treat men as one treats other "material". (Arendt 1958: 188)

Arendt suggests that the more important realm of politics may not be the sphere of governmental policies, upon which the traditional left was so fixated, but the domain of everyday political engagements we have with one another, our efforts to gain mutual recognition of one another.

This in turn is not isolated to the academic sphere. Though a multitude of themes emerged, a central message coming out of the 1995 Million Man March on Washington DC was the need for African American men to recommit to their families and communities. The organizers of the march identified the themes of personal responsibility and civic leadership as the source of positive change. The point here is that political change and fundamental shifts in values do not have to translate into increased government intervention.

For many in cultural studies there is little hope that cultural change will be brought about by official governmental or legal reform. They are rather calling for a kind of policy that amounts to standing up for our rights, to trying to change the way we talk and think about people who are different from ourselves. They are calling for the intervention into our conversations of voices we have excluded. The everyday dialogue which surrounds the market and political sphere is in fact a potent force in the world, capable of shifting the cultural foundations of society.

3   But is cultural studies compatible with economics?

It appears to be the characteristic belief of certain social critics who pursue the nostalgic mode ... that a community prospers ... in proportion to the extent that its members have achieved consensus or that it prospers more as communal norms become more uniform, coherent, and stable. But the well-being of any community is also a function of other and indeed opposed conditions, including the extent of *diversity* of the beliefs and practices of its members and thus their communal resourcefulness, and the *flexibility* of its norms and patterns, and thus their responsiveness to changing and emerging circumstances.

For, of course, with the exception of Paradise and some other transcendental polities, no community can be *immured* from interactions with a changing environment, nor can the heterogeneity of its members be altogether eradicated and their potential conflicts altogether prevented. Where *difference* continuously emerges, it must be either continuously negotiated or continuously suppressed, the latter always at somebody's cost and often enough, it appears, at, in the long run, considerable *communal* cost. Given such sublunary conditions, it is perhaps just as well for "our society" that its norms are a "mélange," that they constantly multiply, collide, and transform each other, that conflicts of judgment are negotiated ad hoc, and that normative authority itself is multiple and recurrently changes hands, variously strengthening and becoming diffuse.

Barbara Herrnstein Smith (1988: 93–4)

Economics today is done as if culture did not matter. Is there a good reason for this? Does economics have reasons to reject cultural studies as either contradictory with, or as irrelevant to, its own findings? This chapter will suggest that the fundamental beliefs of economists are not inherently contradictory with those of cultural studies.

3.1   On different worlds?

But maybe the reason they do not contradict one another is that they simply have nothing to do with one another. The more difficult obstacle to getting economics and cultural studies to talk to each other is not the issue of whether they directly clash but whether they can come into contact at all. Most economists consider what they are doing to be a completely different kind of effort from what goes on in either the theoretical or the empirical work of cultural studies. The sciences explain, most economists contend, the humanities understand. If this distinction holds then the sciences and humanities are not necessarily contradicting each other, but are simply incommensurable discourses. We have already noted that they tend to use fundamentally divergent empirical research methods: statistical empirical work vs. ethnographic and archival-historical studies. Perhaps this is more than a matter of taste about alternative tools, and reflects utterly incompatible forms of research.

And it does at first appear that economics and cultural studies are living on different planets. They describe themselves in terms of opposite aims: find universal laws or identify local differences. They seem to have fundamentally divergent philosophical anthropologies: individualism or communalism. Economists tend to assert that science is value free, while scholars in cultural studies are keen on undermining and subverting the whole idea of value-free objectivity.

And then there is the enormous and obvious ideological contrast between these literatures. One is what the media calls conservative; it sees market solutions to most problems, and lists issues like tax reform and interest rate policy as among the most urgent and interesting questions of our time. The other is just as plainly what the media call leftist; it sees issues such as sexism, homophobia, or racism, as among the most urgent and interesting of our time. One celebrates free markets, the founding fathers, the Enlightenment, and the reason of the individual person, and the other exposes the fallacies of naive rationalism.

Could it be that these literatures are not just different genres, diverse ways of approaching and describing the study of society, in which case they could be usefully compared, but that they speak of different worlds altogether? Could it be that what cultural studies has to say has nothing to do with what economics has to say?

No. We argue that economics and cultural studies are both about our world, including our economy, and that the apparent philosophical divergence is not as deep as it first appears. The slogan "The sciences explain, the humanities understand" (attributed to philosopher Wilhelm Dilthey) is a dubious position that needs to be challenged. It encapsulates the great truce of modernism: dividing the spoils between the sciences and the arts in such a way that both of the "two cultures" are left impoverished. One is unable to understand what it is explaining, the other to explain what it understands.

If we are serious about wanting to strike up a useful conversation between cultural studies and economics, we need to identify promising conversational partners from each side. Not everyone from cultural studies would care to join this conversation, and many economists will certainly avoid it, but there are many on each side who would welcome it, and we need to start with them. It is true that cultural studies includes some "neo-Marxists" whose revisions of traditional Marxism are sometimes superficial (and who therefore continue to demonize markets). But it also includes genuinely transformed "post-Marxists," such as the aforementioned Critical Theorists and cultural populists, who emphasize the decentralizing virtues of market processes. Philosophically the literature includes some deconstructivists who condemn the Enlightenment across the board, rejecting not only its modernist metaphysics, but apparently its faith in any sort of reason and its classical liberal aspirations. But the literature also includes, as we argued earlier, pragmatists, hermeneuticists, and Critical Theorists who, though just as vigorously rejecting Enlightenment metaphysics, seek to renew its faith in reason and freedom, and try to advance its truths in a non-modernist manner (see Palmer 1991a).

There is also more divergence within the economic literature than may at first meet the eye. The official positivist interpretation of what economics is all about, which has reigned for so long in economics textbooks, is not embraced by every economist. There are interpretations of the main achievements of the economics literature that are fully reconcilable with the central themes of much cultural studies scholarship. There are a number of emerging approaches from different schools of thought which challenge all of the above modernistic biases along the lines of what has been called "interpretive social science" (see Rabinow and Sullivan 1987). Hermeneutically oriented economists from such schools as

- Institutionalism and Post-Keynesianism (Benton 1990; Eichner 1978; Hodgson 1988; Parsons 1991; Samuels 1990)
- the Chicago school (McCloskey 1985, 1990, 1997)
- neo-Marxism (Amariglio 1990; Burczak 1996; Cullenberg 1992; Wisman 1990)
- the Austrian school (Addleson 1995; Ebeling 1986; Hayek 1942, 1955; Lachmann 1971, 1991; O'Driscoll and Rizzo 1985; Prychitko 1990a)

are opening up a discourse in a post-modern way that cultural studies would find congenial. Of all the more interpretive approaches to economics, the one we draw on the most here is the Austrian, led by writers such as Ludwig Mises (1949), Friedrich Hayek (1948), Israel Kirzner (1973), and Ludwig Lachmann (1971, 1994). If one widens the net to include such non-mainstream voices from economics, the conversation between cultural studies and economics might get off the ground.

3.2 The universality of economics, the diversity of economic culture

Economics and cultural studies might seem to be incompatible in terms of the issue of universals. A surefire conversation-stopper between economics and cultural studies is the economist's habit of talking about universal laws. Cultural studies strives to present each culture as unique. It focuses on the details of specific norms of behavior, including market behavior, and has little patience for grand theories or universal laws. Since each particular pattern of behavior is a reflection of a specific culture, there is no guarantee that any one pattern, such as a certain kind of market institution, will always emerge. Cultural studies scholars challenge the coherence of the idea of any sort of fixed, cross-cultural essence of human beings that can be called our "nature." Economists occupy the other side of the spectrum. They are not troubled by propositions that in all societies markets and market principles are at work, since these modes of behavior are not taken to arise out of culture, but rather out of human nature itself. It has been common for economics to stress universal principles, for example, that human action is always self-interested, but there is a wide range of meanings of self-interest, some of which are so broad that anybody would agree that self-interest is universal (a point to which we need to return in the next section).

Since self-interest in some sense is taken by economists to be an inherent part of human nature, market principles will be operating wherever there is human society. This universal character of market coordination is said to be the power of economic inquiry. No matter where one finds oneself in the world, there are certain constants that can be counted on. Whether in a Nigerian open market, a car dealership in Ohio, or a black-market trading post in soviet Moscow, self-interest assures predictable and logical results, as market principles are at work in all these contexts.

There is of course plenty of evidence that markets are ubiquitous. Cultural studies would look over this same body of evidence and alert us to the differences among all these markets: the different social assumptions, the bargaining techniques, the price adjustment patterns, the verbal accoutrements of market exchange, and so forth. And the selves in this process are not homogeneous manifestations of an underlying human nature, but are very diverse and are being continually re-constituted on the basis of social interchange. But this is not so much a refutation of economics as it is a healthy dose of ethnographic empiricism that contributes to our understanding of markets.

The linguistic habits of each field make these differences look more categorical than they really are. Economics need not deny the enormous significance of cultural and historical detail in the understanding of markets. In fact most economic historians, empirical economists, and economic anthropologists tend to be aware of the tremendous diversity of market institutions across different societies and historical epochs. If there is a core of universal, abstract theory that economists like to claim is valid across the whole range of human societies, this core does not try to claim much that anybody would find controversial. That demand curves slope downward may be something economists tend to feel very strongly about, but properly understood, it is not something non-economists need to consider as an ethnocentric bias that is open to challenge. It does not imply that what is demanded will be material things rather than spiritual values, or that businesses will necessarily do what they think will bring money profits. It comes down to saying that whatever people want, they want it at less cost in terms of other things they want. *By itself* economic theory is empty of any empirical punch. And yet it is a profoundly useful framework when it is *not* left by itself, that is, when it is put to work on interpreting real historical and cultural phenomena in all their richly diverse detail.

And by the same token, as much as the proponents of cultural studies rail against the universal theorizing they encounter in the social sciences, cultural studies is in fact filled with theory that purports to have an astonishingly broad range of applicability. When Jacques Derrida asserts that written culture has a profound effect on spoken culture, and that we should beware of a kind of "phonocentrism" that privileges the intellectual significance of verbal modes of discourse over written ones, he is not just talking about French literature, but about all human societies which have embraced any form of writing. Much of cultural theory is more general still, discussing the fundamental nature of language itself. When Hans-Georg Gadamer ([1960] 1989) discusses the way in which our thought is shaped by the linguistic traditions into which we are enculturated, he is not referring to the German language, or to European languages, but to all human languages. Cultural studies theory operates at a highly general philosophical level, examining the underlying character of all linguistically constituted human thought, communication, and action. Only when this theory is put to work in the interpretation of specific cultures does the emphasis on the uniqueness of cultural patterns come into play.

And when economics is put to work on specific historical cases it too sheds much of its universalistic garb, and gets down to details of a particular culture's legal rules, marketing networks, credit transactions, etc. (See, for example, Ayittey 1991; Chamlee 1994; Chamlee-Wright 1997; Little 1965, 1973; Landa 1991.) Now it is true, as we have seen, that most empirical work in economics, unlike that of cultural studies, is statistical, surveying large numbers of instances of a certain kind of practice. But this does not reflect any inherent difference, and there is no reason in principle why cultural studies research could not make more use of statistical methods, or why economics could not make more use of ethnographic and archival historical research.

Indeed, would it not be good medicine for both fields to be exposed to the emphasis of the other? Cultural studies scholars could use a dose of economic theory to more clearly see the logic of how the markets they are studying work. Economists could use a dose of ethnographic field work to see how useful their own theoretical framework can be on the ground. By attending to the ethnographic reality of fundamental diversity among markets, economists can see how each culture offers a variety of solutions to solve complex problems of order and coordination. We could notice that policies which work in some settings may have little effect in others. If we consider only the universal aspects of markets as our theoretical guide, we are likely to miss the reasons why this is so.

A dose of ethnography would do much to enrich the economists' own account of economic phenomena. Economists sometimes fool themselves with their own theoretical rhetoric, assuming that the "optimal" choice is an objective matter, when in fact it is dependent on people's perspectives, that is, on culture. Economists can give the false impression that there is only one decision that will be "objectively" profit-maximizing, only one "correct" entrepreneurial move that can be made at any moment in time, that only one strategically sound path will bring profit. Cultural studies reminds us that what one takes to be the "rational" choice depends on the context, and that perspectives can be profoundly different from one another. Economists' stories about market institutions and processes, which tend to repeat themselves in the genre of the equilibrating mechanism working itself out, would be enriched if they were to be retold with some different plot lines, if they were understood as cultural processes, as polysemic processes of mutual interpretation and criticism.

It is not a critique of economic theory that it is "empty" in the sense that much of it is so general it is beyond any possibility of empirical falsification. Nor is it a condemnation of cultural studies that it likes to focus on the details of cultural practices in all their diversity. Beneath the surface, these fields are more complements than rivals.

3.3   Individualism, communalism, and rights

Cultural studies and economics might seem to be irreconcilable on the matter of individualism. Economics proceeds from a philosophical stance it labels "methodological individualism." Its official rhetoric insists that the "fundamental unit" of analysis for economic problems is the choice situation facing the individual human actor. The isolated individual agent, often pictured as Robinson Crusoe on an island, is treated as the basic starting point of analysis (see Kirzner 1963). It is undeniable that a certain kind of "individualism" is an integral part of economic theory. The very core of economic analysis is the examination of what actors consider, from their own subjective point of view, to be their most rational course of action, the means which would best attain the ends sought. This theory is traditionally introduced on the simplified Crusoe level, but rarely is the issue raised as to how unrepresentative of real human action the behavior of an isolated man on an island is.

From the origins of economics and classical liberal thought, "self-interest" has been deployed by economists in three fundamentally different ways: as a general *interpretive* framework, according to which it simply means whatever the actor in question took to be the best course of action; or as part of a substantive proposition, often called the *"invisible hand"* thesis, that when people act primarily with their own interests in mind, unintended social benefits can, under certain conditions, accrue to society; or in a still narrower *instrumental* sense, where each actor is seen to be calculating his own strategic advantages against all other actors, what Habermas called instrumental rationality. Many economists slip into this much narrower notion of self-interest in which action is considered a matter of selfish wealth maximization, and the calculation of strategic advantage.

In the interpretive framework sense, economics is saying only that the concepts of cost and trade-off and so forth can be usefully wrapped around any observable event, and that this is helpful. Altruistic action is self-interested in the framework sense in that the actor sees advantages (in self-esteem or whatever) in making a gift over not making it. Non-calculative behavior, habits, and so forth can all be illuminated by the use of economic categories of choice.

Adam Smith, in formulating his famous invisible hand thesis, pointed out that even those who act on the behalf of others are motivated by self-interest, since it is the approbation of their peers that they ultimately seek in acting charitably towards others. But what Enlightenment liberalism underappreciated was that this "self" that seeks its own interest is not immediately transparent to the individual. Life is, among other things, an exploration of self-discovery, of trying to determine one's identity. Cultural studies can add to the economists' discourse about self-interest by illuminating the social construction of identity. It may, in other words, be one's own self-esteem that one is seeking, rather than the approbation of one's peers.

If the notion of self-interest is taken in its broadest, *interpretive* sense, to include for example, actions aimed at improving people's self-esteem on account of their adherence to fundamental principles, then it should be uncontroversial to claim that self-interest is universal. If it is taken in its narrowest *instrumental* sense, then it is highly controversial, even among economists, to claim that all or even most action is self-interested. It is not difficult to get many economists to admit that most people have "interdependent utility functions" which is an inelegant way to say that individuals are not strictly out for their own strategic advantages against everybody else. In fact, although mainstream economics has often interpreted self-interest in a rather narrow manner, the larger classical liberal tradition and other schools of economics such as the Austrian school use a much broader notion (see Holmes 1995: 42–68).

Cultural studies can agree unreservedly with the interpretive framework sense of the word self-interested, where it is defined broadly enough to include non-selfish and non-calculative actions. Here economics is providing an analytical tool that may help in understanding markets, and this tool is thoroughly empty unless it is put to work on interpreting particular economic circumstances. Here we can see possibilities for collaboration among students of cultural and market processes. And cultural studies can explicitly show how limited the narrower instrumental sense of self-interestedness is, and demonstrate by solid ethnographic work the complex interconnectedness and interdependence of individuals in society.

But what of the more substantive invisible hand thesis? Does it employ a sense of "self-interest" that can withstand the scrutiny of cultural studies? In the invisible hand sense, self-interest is being deliberately contrasted with altruistic behavior, and recognized as a powerful driving force behind trade, prosperity, and social coordination. The thesis is that the complex allocative tasks performed in a market setting are not achieved by virtue of treaty or collective agreement, but are the unintended consequence of individuals following their own self-interest. The diverse plans of countless producers and consumers come into concert with one another not because each deliberately takes the rest of society into account. On the contrary, it is precisely because each participant in the market is taking her "own interest" into account, and thus is equipped with local and often tacit knowledge, that the market is able to achieve the level of social coordination that it does (see Lavoie 1985, 1990a).

To be sure the language of this rhetoric is not apt to sit well with cultural studies scholars. Within the classical liberal tradition, coming out of the Enlightenment, the self-interest which is responsible for the vast benefits that accrue to society is seen as a principal part of "human nature." But shorn of its naturalistic garb, all the invisible hand thesis is saying is that, under appropriate rules and norms of behavior, self-interested action leads to desirable unintended outcomes. It need not deny that a person's self-interest may itself be constructed out of social influences.

For some economists there is perhaps a perceived threat here. A research agenda which investigates the role of culture in the market process might pose a challenge to the supposition some mainstream economists make about the autonomy of individual choice. Since people do not choose their culture, any influence that culture has on the individual offers a challenge to the basic premise that people are rationally responding to incentives according to their own self-interest. In other words, some economists seem to fear that we would be unable to claim that there are systematic results to market behavior if people are "blindly following" custom or ritual rather than "rationally responding" to incentives. If individual responses are based on cultural influences rather than incentives, it is feared, there would be no systematic tendencies in market processes.

But cultural studies scholars would answer that this whole contrast between rational self-interest and culture is misconceived. All rational deliberation takes place within cultural parameters. What serves as an incentive for somebody depends on what the person wants. What seems rational depends on the prevailing culture's understanding of things. Culture is not another factor to be considered in addition to rational incentives, it is the underlying meaning of the specific content of any rational choice.

Within the economics profession the general notion of "rational self-interest" is sometimes used as an excuse to avoid entanglement in the *content* of interests, and the intricacies of culture. The attractiveness of the general theories seduces many into a narrowing of research agendas. Both the mathematical mode of theorizing and the statistical mode of empirical work draw the attention of economists away from the detailed meaning of market exchanges to the actual participants. But ignoring cultural influences on preferences and insisting on merely repeating the abstract thesis that individuals act in their own self-interest is not a necessary stance for economists to take. It is rather another symptom of the economics profession's exaggerated attention to universal theory as opposed to the particulars of empirical reality. Useful theory is that which helps us to render the world more intelligible.

In failing to make ethnographic contact with the culture of markets, we forfeit an opportunity to fill out the skeleton of economic theory with the stuff of everyday market life. From such studies could come a deeper understanding of social institutions and the value systems which are essential components in the development of markets. For example, self-interest cannot guarantee allocative efficiency or overall economic coordination if we are not within the context of a system of private property, or if there are no common communicative standards, or if there is no legal framework within which to resolve disputes and enforce contracts. This is not to minimize or deny the importance of self-interest in establishing the economic order, rather the point here is to recognize that self-interested behavior in the invisible-hand sense takes place in a specific cultural context. Thus, market behavior will reflect the specific social norms, institutions, value systems, and conventions of acceptable behavior that have emerged in that cultural setting. While we can say that all human beings act in a somewhat self-interested manner, no matter what the cultural context, we must also recognize that the content of that self-interested behavior, the entrepreneurial ventures, business training, credit acquisitions, will all be shaped by the specific cultural setting. In short, "self-interest" itself is culturally defined.

The economist's way of talking sounds all wrong to students of cultural studies, who are repelled by talk of universal human nature, and who insist that whatever an "individual" is, it is anything but a fundamental, irreducible starting point. When cultural studies scholars stress that the individual is constituted by the society into which she is born, and when economists insist that on the contrary, society is constituted by the individuals of which it is composed, it looks as if they are in directly opposed metaphysical frameworks that are utterly incompatible. To economists it looks like cultural studies wants to treat individuals as homogeneous embodiments of the culture into which they grow up, and as fully determined by their social context. To cultural studies scholars it looks like economics wants to deny that individual human beings are deeply shaped by their culture.

But most cultural studies scholars do not deny that individual subjects in empirical fact are different from one another, but on the contrary emphasize difference. And while they stress the manner in which individual subjects are influenced by their environment, they generally do not deny that individual actions and ideas in turn shape culture. Similarly most economists are not under the impression that individuals are somehow born with their preferences, and they do not need to argue against the claim that preferences are profoundly shaped by culture or highly interdependent.

Scholars in these fields are speaking utterly different languages from one another, and find mutual understanding difficult, but if you can cut through some of the linguistic barriers, genuine communication is possible. What sounds like a fundamental metaphysical chasm on closer inspection proves to be a difference in emphasis. To be sure, there are philosophical issues of importance here, which we have been referring to as modernist biases. The Enlightenment's individualistic view that the individual is the starting point, or an irreducible unit of analysis, is untenable. Contemporary cultural studies scholarship is united in concluding that the atomistic notion of Man, and the rationalistic notion of Reason have succumbed to the general critique of modernism. Who we are as conscious choosing agents is something that is constituted within processes of social interaction. Preferences are not some sort of irreducible "given" but are shaped by socialization. Rational decision-making is a product of language, which is necessarily a social process that precedes the individual language-speaker (see Hayek 1979, 1988; Madison 1988).

But cultural studies is not unanimous about whether the whole animating spirit of the Enlightenment needs to be rejected. While cultural studies scholars reject the metaphysics of modernism, many cultural studies writers still seek to defend and expand on what has been gained in modernity. The critique of Enlightenment rationalism does not necessarily entail abandoning the basic rational, liberal, cosmopolitan, and democratic ideals of the Enlightenment. The rejection of certain understandings of the nature of individual action and of aprioristic theories of natural rights need not entail the rejection of individual rights. The philosopher Albrecht Wellmer (1991: 228) a leading social theorist in the Habermasian tradition, clarifies the distinction between individualistic and communalistic anthropologies:

> Individualist theories take isolated individuals, characterized by certain natural rights and a goal-oriented rationality, as their starting point . . . Freedom here is basically the freedom to do what I want to do – whatever it is that I want to do . . . Freedom . . . is what is often called "negative freedom."

Wellmer finds the fundamental philosophy of individualism, understood as the Enlightenment rationalist view that individual men and women are atomistic entities, unconnected to society, to have been demolished by communalistic theories that show the rootedness of individuality in socialization processes.

> Communalist theories, in contrast, do not only question the basic anthropological premise of individualist theories, but, together with this

premise, the individualist notion of individual freedom as such. The anthropological premise which is questioned is that the notion of a human individual outside society, an individual who is not constituted as an individual by becoming socialized as a member of an intersubjective form of life, is an adequate starting point for political theory. If, however, human individuals are essentially social individuals, if, in their very individuality, they are constituted and, as it were, permeated by the culture, traditions, and institutions of the society to which they belong, then their freedom as well must have a social character.

The point that individuals are "socially constructed" can be conceded without concluding that negative freedom is merely conventional, or that fundamental rights should be up for debate in the public sphere. Wellmer (1991: 238) goes on to say that the individualists are right that a fundamental regard for "negative freedom," the protection from all sorts of aggressions by others, is a prerequisite for a democratic society.

For some writers in the cultural studies literature the Enlightenment is to be completely rejected, but from the standpoint of contemporary Critical Theory, it is, as Habermas puts it, "an incomplete project." The "rights of man" may not have been consistently applied to all "men" and they may not be bestowed on us by God or Nature. But as Wellmer (1991: 251) puts it, Critical Theorists have not abandoned "the radical libertarian impulses, the moral universalism, and the democratic aspirations that are part of the project of modernity."

The historical record is clear that societies which, under the influence of Enlightenment ideals about negative freedom, respect these "bourgeois liberties" (as Karl Marx dismissively called them) are far more democratic and economically prosperous than those that do not. Wellmer (1991: 230) points out that though the abstract philosophy of individualism may be weak, the communalists have to admit that there seems to be something to this idea of negative freedom.

> Every communalist . . . has to come to terms with the fact that modern bourgeois society is the paradigmatic society of the Enlightenment in the modern world: the only society in which human rights, the rule of law, public freedom, and democratic institutions have to some extent become safely institutionalized.

Moreover, a principled defense of individual rights does not require a metaphysics of individuality, or a celebration of unconstrained selfishness. To say that protecting these rights is a precondition for a free society is not to say that it is a sufficient condition for the good society. A free society need not be populated by atomistic individuals concerned only to protect themselves from aggression by others, or to advance their own self-interest, where this self-interestedness is narrowly understood. A social notion of freedom could itself be understood as part of a unifying ideal for the political culture.

Freedom, in the fullness of the connotations of our language, means not only freedom from coercion by others, but also participation in the "politics" of all the organizations, communities, and other public spaces we are part of: joining in dialogue in the polity, in the public sphere about our common concerns. "There is no reason," Wellmer (1991: 238) says, "to claim that the universalistic principles of natural rights are not 'translatable' into a communalistic conception of political freedom."

Wellmer (1991: 236) draws his basic conception of culture as an "ethical form of life" from Hegel, but turns to Alexis de Tocqueville for his model of freedom.

> Although the historical experience of the decline of the spirit and the institutions of political freedom in postrevolutionary France was the starting point for both Hegel's and Tocqueville's reflections, they turned in opposite directions to look for alternatives: Hegel thought that he had found a viable alternative in a somewhat idealized Prussian monarchy; Tocqueville, by contrast, turned to a study of the second (sic) great revolutionary society of his time: the American society.

And there in America Tocqueville found something that was absent in France and the rest of Europe: "a spirit of freedom that had become a form of ethical life." What Wellmer means by this is that Tocqueville saw that negative freedom is really more than it first appears. Hegel had been concerned about the disunification of civil society, where there are no common projects, but only individuals "protected" from one another. Tocqueville saw that negative freedom was a positive thing, an ideal that can itself become a shared part of political culture, and can unify a society.

> Freedom alone can draw the bourgeois out of their isolation which is a consequence of the independence of their situation, and force them to come closer to each other; freedom ... unites them every day anew by the necessity, to converse with one another in dealing with matters of common concern, to convince each other, and to do favors to each other ... freedom alone offers nobler objects to ambition than the acquisition of wealth and creates the light in which the vices and virtues of men can be seen and judged. (Translated by Wellmer 1991: 237, from the German edition of Tocqueville's *Der alte Staat und die Revolution* [1856] 1968: 13.)

There is no need to postulate an idyllic past in which the sense of community once (before being destroyed by the individualizing effects of capitalism) was paramount, in order to aspire to a better future, in which our sense of community is stronger than it is now. Indeed, the kind of guild system that early capitalism resisted seemed to have been functioning largely as a special-interest monopoly organization, and bore little resemblance to the sort of democratic community most of us would like to see flourish (see for example, Black 1984). There have been at best only occasional approximations of democratic community in human history from which we can draw inspiration. Hannah Arendt liked to refer to the Greek polis, the French resistance to Nazi occupation, and the American revolution as examples of circumstances where people experienced "the political" in the best sense of public action together, action in which a spirit of democratic self-governance was at least partially experienced by at least some of the population.

One can argue that the increase in civil liberties and in respect for individual autonomy that accompanied the growth of markets represents a necessary (but not sufficient) condition for building genuine community. There is no necessary inconsistency between demanding a consistent protection of individual freedoms and also aspiring to more than protection *from* others. Some degree of such protection is a precondition for the emergence of a genuine community in which we can act together *with* others. It is necessary for the emergence of a form of public life in which our mutual responsibilities to one another can be openly and democratically discussed.

Classical liberalism often fought for a consistent defense of civil liberties but rarely developed a positive appreciation of the idea of public life in civil society. But the left has also erred in too quickly identifying the public sphere with a single, governmentally exercised national will, instead of recognizing it as belonging to the culture itself, a fragmented, tension-filled process.

3.4   Ethnocentrism and markets

Another issue over which cultural studies and economics would appear to have irreconcilable differences is the role of market institutions in non-Western societies. Whereas most economists think that the market order is bound to be an important aspect of the historical development in any society, the cultural studies paradigm seems to suggest that this is not necessarily the case. For some the capitalistic markets, which are found throughout the developing world, are to be dismissed as products of Western imperialism. Economics talks about markets as the natural order of any human society, while cultural studies scholars resist this talk of the "natural" in the first place, and many are unpersuaded that markets are necessarily good for non-Western countries.

Indeed the favorite stick with which the left likes to hit economists is the claim that their faith in markets is a bias of our own Western capitalist culture, a sign of unreflective Eurocentrism and logocentrism. Only because we are modernists, children of the European Enlightenment, only because we are so fixated on reason, and efficiency and so forth, do we find markets so beautiful. Markets are understood primarily to be a playground for the wealthy and powerful, not an arena where women or the poor, or for that matter most of the population of non-Western countries, can partake in its advantages. We should not impose our Western sorts of institutions on those who cannot, or perhaps would not want to, occupy that playground.

Since economists have been so intent on defending the grand universality of their theories, they have failed to respond to the left in their own terms. Markets in fact are ubiquitous. They emerge in nearly all the cultures we know of. Is it not the left's distrust of markets, deriving from the legacy of Karl Marx, that harbors a peculiarly Western bias?

Consulting the historical record of vastly divergent cultures suggests that the economic argument in favor of the universality of markets is more persuasive (see, for example, Anderson and Latham 1986; Baechler 1975; Berger 1986; Boettke 1994; Hayek 1954; Rosenberg and Birdzell 1986). The Chinese historian Ssu-ma Ch'ien ([c.145–86 BC] 1961: 477) had already observed the coordinating capacity of the market process over two thousand years ago.

> There must be farmers to produce food, men to extract the wealth of mountains and marshes, artisans to process these things and merchants to circulate them. There is no need to wait for government orders: each man will play his part, doing his best to get what he desires. So cheap goods will go where they fetch more, while expensive goods will make men search for cheap ones. When all work willingly at their trades, just as water flows ceaselessly downhill day and night, things will appear unsought and people will produce them without being asked. For clearly this accords with the Way and is in keeping with nature.

Centuries before Westerners ever set foot on the African continent, intricate long-distance trade networks had developed which connected East to West and North to South as early as 1100 AD. The establishment of local marketplaces, which were the site of cultural as well as economic exchange among neighboring African villages and tribes predates recorded history (see Ayittey 1991). Commerce and trade holds a similar place in Latin American history. By the first century BC, the Mexican city of Teotihuacan was already foreshadowing its eventual blossoming into a vital commercial center. By the fifth century AD, Teotihuacan regularly received merchants from as far away as the Yucatan and Guatemala (Kandell 1988).

Western imperialism certainly cannot account for these early examples of market society. Nor can Western imperialism account for all the contemporary cases of complex market activity. What colonial experience introduced in many third-world countries was cash crop production, in particular through the introduction of colonial taxes payable only in Western currencies (see Moon 1926: 75–96), not markets. The complex domestic markets of Africa, Latin America, and Asia have well established roots in the history and culture of their respective indigenous societies. It appears, then, that no matter what the culture or age, human society has a strong propensity to generate and engage in market activity.

3.5 Popular culture and markets

One sign of the extent to which the left is undergoing a sea change is its revaluation of popular culture. (For some of the interesting ethnographic work that is being done these days on popular culture, see Stewart 1979, 1984; Radway 1984; Tompkins 1985; Willis 1990; and Wilson 1992. For valuable theoretical accounts of the importance of taking popular culture seriously, see Bourdieu 1984, 1993; Smith 1988.) Today ridicule is routinely poured on the attitude that Shakespeare is *inherently* superior to contemporary film. Serious analyses of popular culture, from soap operas to rock music, are all the rage. But popular culture is, almost by definition, culture that is successful in the marketplace. And in fact, the High Art that was so venerated by the New Critics was in its own day popular. Shakespeare was a successful entrepreneur (see the fascinating book on commercial culture by Tyler Cowen 1998). There are deeper implications of this change in attitude among students of culture than probably most have themselves realized. These changes will, we think, significantly alter the ideological landscape.

Paul Willis (1990), one of the leading cultural studies scholars from the Centre for Contemporary Cultural Studies, gives evidence that The Arts, in the sense of what is sometimes called "highbrow" art, are not particularly influential over the ways of thinking of most people, especially not the thinking of the young. If all one considers is elite art forms, the art much of academia itself enjoys, it is easy to conclude that these "cultural" activities are not of much significance in shaping values. Great Art, as opposed to the *mere entertainment* that the masses watch on TV, seems to have little influence over fundamental values.

The fact that the word "popular" is so apt to be taken as an insult, is itself indicative of what have until recently been the prevailing voices in the humanities, whether from conservative or radical sides. Both sides have insisted on maintaining a distinction between the "high" and merely popular arts. The right celebrates the great art of the past, and charges that the Liberal Establishment, and the academic voices that support it, have destroyed our respect for it. The right, as in the New Criticism movement, ask for a return to values, but they seem to mean a turn to *their* values, their culture. The left used to agree that the high arts are superior, and to offer Freudian psycho-sociological "explanations" of why everyday folks have such bad taste or succumb to false consciousness.

The principal critique of popular culture that comes from the traditional left is that of the Frankfurt School. Horkheimer and Adorno ([1947] 1988), for instance, argued that the culture industry systematically dulls the imagination and extends the totalizing effects of industrial capitalism.

[Films] are so designed that quickness, powers of observation, and experience are undeniably needed to apprehend them at all; yet sustained thought is out of the question if the spectator is not to miss the relentless rush of facts. Even though the effort required for this response is semi-automatic, no scope is left for the imagination. Those who are so absorbed by the world of the movie – by its images, gestures, and words – that they are unable to supply what really makes it a world, do not have to dwell on particular points of its mechanics during a screening. All the other films and products of the entertainment industry which they have seen have taught them what to expect; they react automatically. The might of industrial society is lodged in men's minds. The entertainments manufacturers know that their products will be consumed with alertness even when the customer is distraught, for each of them is a model for the huge economic machinery which has always sustained the masses, whether at work or at leisure – which is akin to work. From every sound film and every broadcast program the social effect can be inferred which is exclusive to none but is shared by all alike. The culture industry as a whole has modeled men as a type unfailingly reproduced in every product. All the agents of this process, from the producer to the women's clubs, take good care that the simple reproduction of this mental state is not nuanced or extended in any way. (Horkheimer and Adorno [1947] 1988: 126–7)

Horkheimer and Adorno argued that the culture industry serves the interests of the business establishment by feeding the consumer a steady diet of mind-numbing entertainment. Mass industrial culture stupefies the public into seeking identity and fulfillment through greater and greater consumption. Further, mass culture reduces the public's ability to see its own oppression, thereby maintaining the power and status of the business establishment.

But the academic left within the humanities is no longer so comfortable with this condemnation of popular culture. Contemporary historical research and art criticism have torn apart the whole distinction between high and low art. The strongest voice today in cultural research is speaking up for the folk art, the art that had heretofore been ignored by the official guardians of the literature. There are art forms that are central to the everyday lives of the vast majority of people, and when academia stops its sneering long enough to pay attention, they discover "greatness" in the art of the everyday folks. True, the Art of the elite critics, the art that is promoted by the official Art Institutions that have been the primary concern of government policies, has little impact on the public's values, but the arts that *do* have a major impact are those that are called "popular," those that are products of the spontaneous market.

Popular art is not only popular in the sense of reaching a large national or international market, but also in reaching small localized markets, the art of the MTV mass market, or of the local rock performances in the pubs of Liverpool. But in either case it is popular in the sense of *reaching*, of reaching everyday folks, and not just the *cognoscenti*, of reaching significant groups of people in a way that becomes central to their lives. Which is to say, the popular tends to be *commercially viable,* whether in niche or mass markets. The popular world of art is seeking a paying market, not largesse from the official institutions of the Art Establishment. Willis (1990: 129) links the turn to popular culture with a re-interpretation of the significance of markets.

> It will certainly seem heretical for many to find the main seeds for everyday cultural development in the commercial provision of cultural commodities rather than in the finer practices of art, politics or public institutions. But we must start from unpalatable truths or from no truths at all.

Consider the ideological importance of the on-going revaluation of commercial markets that has been taking place among leading components of the humanities world. Not so long ago "The People's Art" connoted the hollow rhetoric of Socialist Realism, the utopian promise of enlisting the leading intellectuals in a grand project to create a whole new art for the State. Today the art that succeeds in the commercial market is more likely to be treated as the art of the people. Students of culture are increasingly focussing on the art that is developed in production for the market, production that sometimes makes for financial success in appealing to large segments of the consuming public. Willis (1990: 129) says:

> The "arts" are a dead letter for the majority of young people. Politics bore them. Institutions are too often associated with coercion or exclusion and seem, by and large, irrelevant to what really energizes them. "Official culture" has hardly recognized informal everyday culture, still less has it provided usable materials for its dialectical development. Worse, the "holiness" of "art" has made the rest of life profane. . . . At least the anarchic market has been the great leveller.

Simon During (1993a: 18–19) warns that "a 'cultural populism' which can celebrate Madonna . . . is subtly, if unconsciously, connected to the promotion of market forces." But he quickly adds that he is not saying that when cultural studies ethnographers enter into cultural markets they will necessarily be co-opted. One gets the sense that many cultural studies scholars are almost embarrassed about having to admit that "in principle, cultural markets can provide a variety of products, pleasures, and uses, including transgressive and avant-garde ones," and need to make sure their accounts of popular art are "nuanced" enough so that they are not misunderstood to be artistically celebrating everything that achieves market success. Thus During writes:

> Indeed the expansion and differentiation of cultural markets have been tremendously fruitful in all kinds of ways – they are perhaps the major force that will keep cultural studies alive. But cultural populism requires a very nuanced account of the relations between cultural markets and cultural products, and between culture and politics, in order to convincingly celebrate (some) popular culture as "progressive."

The left has been undergoing a major transformation over the past twenty or so years, one which suggests the possibility that it is beginning to take a profoundly different attitude toward markets. The left is showing signs of advancing itself to a new Post-Marxist stage, to a recognition that market processes can be and often are profoundly liberating and democratic forces in social change. While many of the best scholars on the left remain skeptical about "free markets," understood as impersonal forces moving atomistic individuals, they are beginning to see markets as having a fundamentally progressive, liberating side.

Were cultural studies scholars to take up the study of market processes, they would have a great deal that is useful to say to economists. For example, they might help us to think through the issues we take up in the next chapter about the cultural conditions for economic prosperity, including a better substantive understanding of what any given culture considers prosperity to be. Or they may have much to say to help us to think through the issues we take up in Chapter 6 about the nature of moral decision-making within business enterprises.

But they are not saying it. Cultural studies has not yet touched on substantive economic questions such as this. Why? They are left unexplored because the methods and language of economists are so foreign to cultural studies scholars, and because many of them have not yet outgrown the legacy of the Marxian condemnation of markets.

Freed of its ideological blinders, the cultural studies approach could offer economists just the kind of alternative methodological orientation that they need to transcend the limitations of Robinson Crusoe models, and really begin to take culture into account. It makes change intelligible, as something that grows out of history, yet it permits radical, non-mechanistic change. The theory of entrepreneurship and the market process could more fully account for economic change if it were built on the work of the cultural studies movement. Or so we will argue in the next chapter.

4 How does culture influence economic development?

A culture is an aggregate of divergent and contradictory pictures, and each picture is true.

Hidetoshi Kato (cited in Kotkin 1992: 10)

Agrarian reform, economic reform, financial reform, constitutional reform? Certainly Brazil needs reforms and achievements of all kinds – railways and highways, hydroelectric energy, . . . but what is really needed is a reform within the Brazilian mind. Don't have any illusions: without a reform within the mind . . . that makes us shape within ourselves, not only intellectually but . . . above all emotionally, a radical shift of concepts and attitudes about life, Brazil, and the universe . . . we shall continue to be what we are: a country that progresses but does not ennoble itself, a country without a message for the world, a disorganized collectivity that lacks moral initiative and public spirit . . . that permanently awaits miracle workers or caudillos to solve the problems that only spiritually, morally, and organically integrated communities can really resolve.

Clodomir Vianna Moog (1964: 198), cited in Harrison (1992: 50)

Why are some societies better able to use their natural endowments of resources? Why do some readily embrace growth-friendly institutions and others resist them? We will claim that one of the most important elements in economic development is something that sounds thoroughly subjective: the culture. If there is a spirit of enterprise, a set of stories or images in the culture that celebrate some form of entrepreneurial creativity, then economic prosperity is more likely. If you want to get a sense of whether a community is apt to grow wealthier, we are suggesting you find out what stories they tell, what myths they believe, what heroes they admire, what metaphors they use. Economic development is, at its heart, a cultural process.

How does a "culture" – in the anthropologist's sense of a context, a shared set of attitudes and values which constitutes what people find meaningful and significant in life – influence economic performance? This is the kind of question that Max Weber investigated in his masterful two volume work *Economy and Society*, and that Hernando de Soto (1988) explored in his study of the informal sector in Peru. It is what, under an unmistakably Weberian influence, Peter Berger and his colleagues at the Institute for the Study of

Economic Culture have been investigating at length in regard to Asian, Latin American and African development (see Brigitte Berger 1991; Martin 1990; Redding 1990). We cannot undertake such detailed ethnographic work here, but what we would like to do is clarify a bit how best to pose this question.

Cultural conservatives discuss culture in terms of identifying, and perhaps reinforcing, the hegemony of a unitary "national culture," say, American Values. We want to encourage a different approach. Ethnographic research that is sensitive to the subtle difficulties of understanding, such as is found in the cultural studies literature, can flesh out the details of the economists' own theories. One example is the issue of entrepreneurship. Economists have been asking the question in the abstract: What is the "essence" of entrepreneurship? In fact some very useful understanding of some fundamental aspects of entrepreneurship has come from the work of Joseph Schumpeter, Ludwig Mises, Israel Kirzner and others. But it might be argued that the theoretical development of the notion of entrepreneurship has reached something of an impasse. Perhaps a more useful direction for research to take in order to develop such theories further is that of examining the specific local cultural contexts of actual entrepreneurial activity. Here one finds some interesting differences, for example, between the contexts of American, Japanese, and Chinese entrepreneurship, which we will examine later in this chapter.

4.1   Which culture prospers? Comparative cultural advantage

Development economists such as P.T. Bauer (1954, 1957, 1971, 1984) and new institutional economists such as Douglass North (1989, 1990, 1994) have made significant strides in moving economics away from the institution-less world of mainstream economics. Their contributions have centered around identifying institutional structures conducive to lower transactions costs, the expansion of trade, and improved economic performance. The next step, we think, is to understand the cultural processes which support the institutions so crucial to economic performance. Such a pursuit is not at odds with the work of Bauer or North. Both scholars have recognized the significance of culture within the market process. Bauer (1954) recognized the customary dimension of informal markets in his study of West African trade. Douglass North in his work with Arthur Denzau (1994), argues that

> ...[i]deas matter; and the way ideas are communicated among people is crucial to theories that will enable us to deal with strong uncertainty problems at the individual level. For most of the interesting issues in political and economic markets, uncertainty, not risk, characterizes choice-making. Under conditions of uncertainty, individuals' inter-pretation of their environment will reflect their learning. Individuals with common cultural backgrounds and experiences will share reasonably convergent mental models, ideologies, and institutions; and individuals

with different learning experiences (both cultural and environmental) will have different theories (models, ideologies) to interpret their environment... [I]n order to understand decision making under such conditions of uncertainty we must understand the relationship of the mental models that individuals construct to make sense out of the world around them, the ideologies that evolve from such constructions, and the institutions that develop in a society to order interpersonal relationships. (Denzau and North 1994: 3–4)

Though hinted at here and there, the study of the cultural foundations of institutions and economic performance is not yet a well developed line of inquiry within the new institutionalist school, and is utterly invisible to most of the economics profession. Much more work is needed if we are to understand the cultural processes which underlie institutions and market processes.

The way not to ask the question about the relationship between culture and economic prosperity is to score different "national cultures" against a set of universal cultural strengths to see which one wins, that is, which one best promotes economic development. Such "cultural nationalism" begs important questions about what economic prosperity really means in different cultural contexts, and equates culture with some sort of (probably mythical) averaged-out, prevailing, national consciousness. Neither the notion of a single, homogeneous national culture, nor that of a universal list of cultural strengths, nor even that of a single objective definition of economic prosperity, will stand up to close scrutiny.

4.1.1 The meaning of economic development

Our first task is to clarify what we mean by "economic development." Many of the scholars who are drawn to cultural studies and economics share a serious concern about poverty in the world, so one might expect that they would be talking with one another about how culture might shape development. But the communicative challenges are so great here that it is difficult even to begin the discussion, for example, to even agree about what "economic development" is, much less on whether in some sense culture is relevant to it. Economists refer unreflectively to economic growth or development as if these words stood for obvious and uncontested objective things, but the study of culture makes one alert to the radical diversity of human meanings and practices, and thus to the fact that "prosperity" can mean radically different things to different people. We need to take seriously the culture's own notions of what prosperity or "wealth" is, realizing that for some it may mean more leisure time, for others more technological gadgets, for some cleaner air, for others a better sense of community, for some more cars, for others cheaper bread. Indeed, for any individual person it must mean a whole set of such things in a complex pattern, dozens of criteria with widely different weights assigned to each.

Yet we think there is overall pragmatic agreement about roughly what we mean by "improvements in the economy's performance," and few of us would have any trouble deciding between the Democratic Republic of Congo's (DRC) or Hong Kong's economic performance over the past couple of decades. Controversies exist over what to do to try to respond to *poverty* problems, and over how best to improve the economy's ability to generate *wealth*, but there is strong agreement that we can, for practical purposes, tell the difference, and that the one is bad and the other good.

For our purposes we would like to characterize the economic development process as a discovery procedure, as a process in which the coordinating capacity of the market improves, leading to an increase in the complexity of the structure of production of goods and services, which in turn improves the living standards of most of its participants. We contend that the economy's wealth-generation process, its ability, roughly speaking, to produce more output of valued goods and services, for the same level of input of labor and other scarce resources, is real, and is really important. Even after duly considering all the difficulties of aggregation, we need to acknowledge that there is some meaning to the everyday observation that our ability to afford more of whatever it is we want, varies with different locations and times, and changes for the better in certain reasonably identifiable circumstances. For the purposes of this study we would like to take as given the notion that we can often tell whether an economy is prospering or declining, and that research in economic development can contribute something by elucidating conditions that would be conducive to a prosperity-generation process.

Aggregate statistics, such as per capita gross domestic product (GDP) levels and growth rates are useful tools to compare economic conditions across countries and time. We cannot silence the sincere complaints of the Romanians about the poor performance of their economy with hair-splitting about the imprecision of GDP measurements or the diversity of human tastes. Their poor are not, in general, simply choosing to consume more leisure time, they are desperately struggling for an adequate material standard of living. We are not interested here in debates about whether an estimate of the DRC's per capita GDP growth from 1980–1994 at negative 3.7% or an estimate of Hong Kong's for the same period at positive 5% (Gwartney, Lawson and Block 1996: xxiii) are precisely accurate, but we have no doubt that such numbers tell us something. Such statistics give us at least a rough sense of whether the country is "prospering" or not, and in the extreme cases it is obvious enough from anecdotal evidence whether an economy is doing very well or very badly.

GDP statistics are not enough. By themselves they beg the question of what counts as "prosperity." The "basic needs" literature within development economics has already criticized the use of growth statistics as a proxy for development (Ghosh 1984). Basic needs theorists argue that true development has more to do with the average person's access to clean water, health care, balanced nutrition, and education than to the aggregate level of

GDP. Further, many development theorists have pointed out that per capita growth rates often obscure the picture of development, when the overwhelming bulk of resources are held in the hands of an elite few.

Moreover, while avoiding poverty and achieving some degree of material wealth is in itself a rather uncontroversial shared goal, there is no reason it should become an all-embracing goal of public policy. We do not embrace the "wealth-fetishism" one finds in some of the economic development literature, the notion that whatever increases material living standards is good. Economic development policy agendas have been frequently used, for example, to justify the violation of fundamental democratic freedoms. In our own view public policy should not be directed at targeting some sort of growth level for the whole society, but should be primarily concerned with protecting the civil and economic freedom of individual citizens. As the television ad puts it, there is no law that says you need to contribute every day to the Gross National Product. It is their own business if the citizens of Ruritania decide to live for today, or go back to nature, or do other things that reduce reported national incomes.

The subjectivist approach to economics, which is at the center of this study, helps us to identify additional problems with the use of growth statistics as a proxy for development. First, the actual makeup of GDP is just as important as the rate at which GDP is rising (or falling). For example, the sale of locks, bars, guns, and other anti-theft devices count towards a growing GDP. But the growth of such industries may be indicative of general social decay in which theft and violent crime are on the rise. Depending upon the content of GDP, its growth may or may not indicate a better overall quality of life. Secondly, aggregate growth statistics often do not capture the structural health of the economy. If half of GDP is the result of political choices, rather than the free and voluntary market choices of individuals, then a growing GDP does not necessarily indicate a healthier economy. Aggregate statistics may serve a useful purpose, but they can never tell a complete story.

Roughly, though, we know "economic development" when we see it. We can tell, for example, without claiming to measure such things precisely, that at the beginning of the 21st century there is severe poverty throughout most of the society in Romania, and relative wealth in Canada. In principle, it could conceivably be that what people want is ascetic serenity, purity of the soul, and a simple life, so that increasing the economy's capacity to generate wealth is considered a bad thing, or at least irrelevant to their subjective meaning of "wealth." But when you see people starving you can pretty much tell that food is high enough on their priority list, and that the problem is that they simply cannot afford enough of it.

What most people around the world have tended to want in practice is increases in wealth that can be translated into more leisure time, better working conditions on the job, or more or better consumption of goods and services. There is nothing sacred about what people currently want, and there is nothing wrong with any of us as individuals trying to change people's minds about what we think they ought to want. But at the same time we need to respect the empirical fact that most people today tend to want something that can be roughly called material wealth. Experience suggests that there are certain developmental processes, which some countries have undergone to a greater extent than others, by which people come to better afford more of whatever it is they want. We think that we have a good enough understanding of economic development processes to be able to explain fairly well why Romanians have less of this thing called wealth than Canadians, and to identify in broad terms what sorts of things Romanians could do to improve their economy's performance.

So let us agree for the moment that having more, rather than fewer goods and services available for consumption, or better wages or working conditions, or more leisure time, or let us just call it having a "higher standard of living," is an essential piece of what we mean by the relative economic success of a country. Yet, increases in output are more the effect of the development process, rather than its essence. For the purposes of this study we mean by the "development process" one in which human society is able to grow in complexity, because the coordinating capacity of the market has grown (Hayek 1988: 38–47). As social institutions such as property rights, contract law and conventional rules of business evolve, the division of knowledge and labor potentially become extended. The development of credit and financial markets, for example, represent the growth of a certain kind of specialized knowledge. Lenders and investors become increasingly knowledgeable of and responsive to the conditions that affect the overall stability of the market. The development of this specialized knowledge allows for greater complexity in terms of the kinds of projects that can be pursued across time and distance. It becomes increasingly commonplace that producers and consumers of the same goods have no awareness of the other's identity. This is not to suggest that face-to-face interaction becomes unimportant in a developing market. Rather, the point is that individuals increasingly make use of and benefit from the specialized knowledge others possess. Greater productivity and material wealth are then the result of this process.

Like any definition of economic development, the one offered here is informed by a particular disciplinary and cultural perspective. It is important to acknowledge that the values implied in our characterization of economic progress may not be universally shared. An Amish community, for instance, may place a higher value on master craftsmanship than the benefits associated with the division of labor and knowledge. Yet, any characterization of the development process will inevitably run into limitations of this kind. If we are to take the subjectivist approach seriously, we must recognize that "progress" will be a culturally defined concept. But we think that the characterization of economic development as a process by which rules and institutions are able to coordinate increasingly complex productive arrangements is a reasonable and helpful starting point.

4.1.2 Cultural nationalism

Culture, as Max Weber understood a century ago, and as the cultural studies literature shows today, is a rich set of diverse and complexly interwoven strands and conflicting tendencies. For cultural nationalism "our culture" (mainstream, middle class, American, etc.) is pitted against "theirs." If there is one thing cultural studies scholarship has demonstrated decisively it is that any nation (and especially the United States) is not really a unitary culture, but a system of interacting cultures. For example, Republican American values represent only some of the many strands that the diverse culture of North American society contains. One thing the contemporary world does not need is more rhetoric to inflame the already overheated notions of "national culture" that pit us against them.

The cultural nationalist way of talking about culture is often little more than a weapon with which cultural conservatives can beat various ethnic groups and other subcultures it does not tolerate into submission. When, for example, William J. Bennett and Lawrence E. Harrison address issues of culture, they are primarily trying to promulgate their own conservative American values, not trying genuinely to understand the specific strengths and weaknesses that each cultural system contains.

In his *Index of Leading Cultural Indicators* (1994: 8–9) William J. Bennett, former Drug Czar and Secretary of Education, tries to gauge the extent to which our culture has undergone "social decomposition." Now we can admit that some of what he means by social decomposition does in fact represent an erosion of values that are conducive to economic prosperity. When family structures grow fragile, when the value of the work ethic is undermined, when respect for property and law is lost, the society's capacity for economic prosperity is correspondingly weakened. But Bennett seems to mean by decomposition the extent to which values stray from the particular form of prosperity-enhancing values that represent what he considers the good-old fashioned, Anglo-American middle-class culture that he likes. Uncomfortable with a culture that places higher value than he would on "things like self-expression, individualism, self-realization, and personal choice," he uses his research on culture to assert the superiority of middle-class American culture over that of all deviations from it. Such attempts to homogenize American culture into a single, national consciousness can only aggravate the anxieties America's diverse cultures already have about one another.

Or take a book that actually presents itself as arising from the Weberian tradition, Lawrence E. Harrison's *Who Prospers? How Cultural Values Shape Economic and Political Success.* Harrison is interesting here in that he represents neither of the scholarly disciplines we have critically surveyed in the previous chapters, cultural studies and economics, and so lacks the defects and the strengths of both disciplines. His book does not suffer from the systemic misdirection both economics and cultural studies have often had, in presuming that markets are objective forces, external to human meaning, but tries to treat cultural values and market performance together. Yet it also lacks the strengths that economics can supply in terms of a more solid understanding of the way markets work, and that cultural studies could supply in terms of a better appreciation of the nature of culture.

Although Harrison's work, like that of Bennett, makes a number of insightful observations about many of the kinds of cultural values that are conducive to economic development, his analysis is severely crippled by a tendency to homogenize the societies whose cultures he is studying. This tendency to try to undertake large-scale comparisons of grossly aggregated cultural groupings can be overcome by drawing from the strengths of the fields of economics (for example, its notion of comparative advantage) and cultural studies (for example, its notion of fragmentation). The upshot of the critique of economics and cultural studies should not be that we abandon these fields, but that we deploy what is good in each to correct for the deficiencies of the other.

4.1.3　*Values conducive to economic development*

In his introductory chapter Harrison (1992: 16–19) draws from an Argentine journalist, Mariano Grondona, who laid out a binary opposition between "development-prone" and "development-resistant" cultures, and identified some twenty factors that one could look for to determine whether any given culture is growth friendly or not. It may be worthwhile to quote from Harrison's paraphrasing of Grondona's thesis, not only because there is an element of truth here, but also to suggest how misleading this way of setting up the issue can be. Here are the dozen factors Harrison lists:

- *Religion* explains and justifies success in a development-prone culture. In a development-resistant culture, religion relieves or explains suffering.
- *Wealth* is *created* as the product of human initiative and effort in the favorable culture. Wealth is the natural or physical resources that *exist* in the resistant culture, and life is a struggle to acquire (or redistribute) it.
- *Competition* is viewed in a progress-prone culture as a positive force that promotes excellence and enriches the society. The resistant culture discourages competition as a form of aggression that threatens the stability and solidarity of the society, in part because it nurtures envy.
- *Economic justice* demands saving and investment for the benefit of future generations in the progressive culture. In the resistant culture, economic justice demands equitable distribution to the current generation.
- *Labor* is a moral, social duty and a central form of self-expression and satisfaction in a favorable culture. In a resistant culture it is a burden, a necessary evil; real pleasure and satisfaction are attainable only outside the workplace.
- *Heresy*, or dissent, is crucial to progress, reform, and the search for truth in the favorable culture, which encourages innovation. The

heretic is a criminal who threatens stability and solidarity in the resistant culture.

- *Education* nurtures inquisitiveness and creativity in a favorable culture. In a resistant, traditional culture, it transmits orthodoxy.
- *Pragmatism, rationalism, empiricism, and utilitarianism* are central values in a favorable culture; threats to stability, solidarity, and continuity in a resistant culture. Tradition, emotion, and chance substitute for rationality, with stagnating consequences.
- *Time focus* is the manipulable future in the favorable culture. The resistant culture focusses on the past, and the concept of future is one of destiny, reflecting a fatalistic world view.
- *The world* is a setting for action and achievement in a favorable culture; one approaches it with optimism. In the resistant culture, the world is controlled by irresistible forces . . .; one approaches it with pessimism, if not fear.
- *Life* is "something I will do" in the favorable culture. In the resistant culture life is "something that happens to me."
- *Optimism* is nurtured in the favorable culture. In the resistant culture, survival is the goal and pessimism the mood.

There are some truths in this list, though they are perhaps somewhat obvious ones. When people put a high value on creativity or savings, powerful economic rewards can result. Certain growth-friendly attitudes, such as considering work a duty or even a form of self-expression as opposed to a burden, are likely to make the individuals who have them more inclined to attain economic prosperity than the opposite attitude. Attitudes toward wealth that are less oriented toward envy of what others have, and more toward creating wealth for oneself, will be conducive to economic development. Willingness to invest in the future promotes the accumulation of wealth.

Yet, all of these categories including the idea of "wealth" itself, cry out for clarification and interpretation. The last four factors for growth-friendliness, for example, basically say that it is better to be optimistic than fatalistic. Yet, what exactly is a culture's approach to fatalism or optimism? There is a certain fatalism in the Calvinism Weber thought he had found behind Western economic development, and a different one in the Confucianism many find behind East Asian prosperity. There could be optimism in cultures that value leisure so highly that they exhaust their society's accumulated capital. Is deep respect for the past necessarily a weakness of a culture – a hindrance to economic prosperity? Perhaps yes, in a culture where respecting the past means that new agricultural techniques are never explored. In another context, however, respecting the past may carve out a place of honor for those who preserve history and tradition. In such a circumstance, the productive potential of the elderly may be more readily recognizable, for instance, as caretakers of young children. The point is that outside of any context, we cannot know if any particular item on Harrison's checklist will inhibit or enable prosperity.

Cultural nationalism asks the wrong question. The research mode here should not be to formulate a binary categorization of a culture – Is it optimistic or not? – but to qualitatively examine specific cultural advantages on their own terms. Within every society are competing definitions of economic prosperity, and each has a heterogeneous array of conflicting cultural tendencies that resist aggregation. The question is posed as if the issue were to compare different countries in terms of their dominant cultural values, when we would argue that the real question is, which among the various values found in different national cultures (sometimes, it is worth stressing, in competition with other values) are the ones whose cultivation would lead to what people would agree is economic prosperity. Ultimately it seems to us that Harrison and other cultural conservatives ask important questions about the relationship between values and economic success, questions that desperately need asking, but pose them so poorly that we end up learning little from the asking.

4.1.4   *Checklist ethnography*

Harrison's list of good values amounts to a rather lame set of homilies, and his summaries of thousand-year-old cultures in three paragraphs are breathtakingly simplistic. What we have is really only a skeleton of an account of the role of culture in economic performance. We learn little about even the bare bone truths that are contained in Harrison's writings, because he does not do anything with them. In trying to survey so many diverse national cultures, this kind of research fails to engage with any particular culture at the level of detail cultural phenomena demand. It merely articulates the issue in a single, abstract sentence – Are they pro-savings or not? – and then attempts to go through the checklist, in effect keeping score on a dozen diverse cultures to see how many come out on the "resistant" or the "favorable" side.

Aside from fueling resentment among different cultures, nothing much follows from scoring better in such contests. Without saying more about what policy implications follow, keeping score on national cultures in this manner does little but offend the cultures that come out losers. Even if it did make sense to "score" a whole nation's culture on a some sort of universal growth-friendliness scale, and even if one country's score were higher in all measurable dimensions, what, from the point of view of economic development, would follow from this? Sometimes cultural nationalism underlies the discussions of whether we might import cultural values from societies that, so to speak, score well. Can Americans benefit from embracing Japanese management practices, or Chinese educational customs, in order to mimic their success? We return to this question in the next section.

Some cultural conservatives including Harrison want to use such assessments of national cultures as a basis of immigration policy. Should we allow more Vietnamese immigrants rather than Mexicans because they score higher on our index of leading cultural indicators? To the extent that national income statistics can measure such things, it might look like our GDP has benefited more from the per capita economic contribution of one group than another. But so what? What kind of politics is it that excludes people from our borders on this kind of basis? What kind of politics identifies human beings by the address they happen to come from, and calculates how wealthy this group would make us, in order to decide whether they have the right to come and live here or not? Is this not the very worst sort of "wealth fetishism" that compromises fundamental civil liberties against the idol of some measure of national income? When whole cultures are assessed in this checklist fashion, and when individual members of cultural groups are evaluated not on their individual merits but on their group's presumed score, one can see the dangers of this approach.

This is what comes from a social scientific theory that is too thin to do the job. Cultural nationalism resorts to categorizing and counting things, when it should spend some effort on understanding what it is counting. It is a mistake to try to understand the cultural elements of a society by first characterizing the overall growth-friendliness of "The Culture As a Whole", that is, treating the nation as the unit of analysis, and "its" culture as a national trait that one can rank as more or less growth-friendly in comparison to those of other nations. Indeed the nation-state is both too big and too small a unit of analysis. As shown in Joel Kotkin's work on *Tribes,* by which he means cultural networks that transcend national boundaries, a culture can be larger or smaller than any particular nation-state. The main point is that the nation-state is not the appropriate unit.

We are not trying to answer the question of which national cultures are most conducive to economic prosperity – whether, say, German culture, as a whole, is more or less likely to generate economic prosperity than American culture, as a whole. This approach obscures the heterogeneity of each culture, reducing cultural studies to a crude sort of Values Nationalism, and ends up unhelpfully comparing apples and oranges. Nor are we arguing a position of cultural relativism, however, by which all cultures are uncritically accepted as being no more or less conducive to prosperity than any other. Relativism also obscures the inherent heterogeneity within and among cultures. How can social scientists account for cultural differences, if we are banned from making any pronouncements about the effects of those differences? The position we are taking here is that each culture carries with it advantages particular to its own context, which might serve to advance economic development. Yet, those advantages will vary according to time and place. Thus, the question we need to ask is: Which elements of American culture (or of this or that particular subculture of American society) constitute its "comparative cultural advantages," and which (probably different) elements of German culture constitute *its* advantages?

4.1.5   Comparative cultural advantage

Each society has cultural advantages which will support varying aspects of market coordination to varying degrees. As Peter Berger suggests, "Two countries with a comparative advantage in two different products can trade the products to their mutual benefit. Perhaps cultural factors operate in the same manner" (Berger and Hsaio 1988: 11). Each society has within its grasp a unique repertoire of "cultural resources." Nature endows some societies with rich oil deposits and others with fertile soil. Similar to these natural resources, culture provides some societies with a kinship network conducive to building complex credit markets and other societies with a strong work ethic. Just as markets will develop differently according to their specific natural resources, they will also develop differently according to their cultural resources. As Douglass North (1990: 44) recognized, culture establishes a path dependence in the evolution of institutions and economic development itself. For instance, capital accumulation takes place in starkly different ways depending on whether it is within West Africa, Japan, the United States, or an overseas Chinese community, because the cultures which support such institutions differ dramatically.

The typical entrepreneur in the Chinese context is the sole proprietor, whereas the typical entrepreneur within Japanese culture is the team player. Young women are brought up to be entrepreneurs in West Africa, quite unlike the Western norm which encourages the male entrepreneur. Weber argues that the culture of Protestantism inspires the hard work and asceticism necessary for economic growth. Many argue that certain interpretations of Confucianism are the cultural inspiration for Asian economic progress.

To the extent that some institutional policies succeed in promoting economic growth and prosperity in one society, there may be important limitations on the wider applicability of those same policies in other contexts, as Cornell and Kalt (1995) found in their comparative study of Native American economic development. The same constitutional structure was imposed upon both the Apache and the Sioux in the 1930s by the Indian Reservations Act, yet the records of economic performance are dramatically different. Cornell and Kalt argue that the social and economic success of the Apache is due largely to the fact that the indigenous governance structure among the Apache closely matched the constitution that was imposed upon them. Yet indigenous governance among the Sioux is far more decentralized than the constitutional order imposed by the Indian Reservations Act. This lack of symmetry has been a major contributing factor in the economic stagnation and social decay that has taken place within Sioux communities. While a highly centralized constitutional order works in one cultural context, it falters in another. Similarly, the success a set of policies might enjoy in one context may not have the supporting cultural resources needed to allow the new policies to take hold.

As essential as they are, free trade and private property rights are no guarantee of economic progress. They may be necessary conditions, but are not sufficient to guarantee prosperity. The culture must be one which in general supports commerce and entrepreneurship, but once again, the particular manner in which the spirit of enterprise can be encouraged will be culturally specific. Western child-rearing techniques which reinforce the value of self-reliance may tend to foster bold entrepreneurial behavior in adulthood. Kinship structure among many African tribes provides the networks through which business people can acquire training and start-up capital. Confucian philosophy which values long-term planning over short-sighted results may in part account for the high savings rates in some Asian societies. Different societies can emphasize varying aspects of markets by drawing upon their unique comparative cultural advantage.

Ever since David Ricardo's clear articulation of the Law of Comparative Advantage it has been understood by economists that the logic applies to relative advantages, and not merely absolute advantages. If a doctor is better than a receptionist at both serving as a receptionist and performing heart surgery, it does not follow that the doctor should fire the receptionist and try to do both jobs. Even if it were the case that producers in Japan were better at producing in each and every industry than producers in Bolivia, all would still benefit from specializing in those production activities in which they had *relative* strengths. The issue is not "inter-country" comparison, but "within-country" comparison. It is not whether some kind of aggregated conglomerate of the whole country's values is better than that of another country, but whether the relative cultural strength within a country is, say, its work ethic or its propensity to save; its trust networks or its attitude toward creativity.

This exposes cultural nationalism to be rather misleading. Even if the checklist could be done well, and even if a culture were judged to have "worse values" across the whole checklist, it is difficult to see what would follow from this. From a comparative advantage perspective, a culture *must* have a relative cultural advantage, no matter how poorly it scores in absolute checklists. The interesting question in regard to comparative advantage is which of a society's cultural strengths are those that can help it promote its own development, as this culture understands what development means. The issue in economic comparative advantage is not which country, say Mexico or the U.S., is better in more things, but which of each culture's strengths are those most suitable for *it* to focus on. Mexicans are not playing a sporting match against the U.S.; they are engaging in mutually beneficial trade. Mexicans should not care about keeping score; they should work on identifying which elements of their culture are the most promising for them to cultivate in order to achieve what they would consider to be prosperity.

The economists' understanding of comparative advantage is a marvelously general notion, as applicable to cultural as it is to material resources, but, like much of economics, it is also crying for some flesh on the bone. What cultural studies could provide here is the specific details of any particular culture's comparative advantages, from which we might gain insights into its likely paths toward economic prosperity. It could help us in the always difficult job of appreciating the differences in another culture, and avoiding the ever-present tendency we have of presuming that our own culture's manner of doing things is the only possible way they can get done. It could help us to accomplish a better reading of the world's cultures, and to find in them possibilities by which their economies can attain emergent patterns of performance which their own participants would call prosperous. It could add to the *general* understanding economists have of the institutional circumstances that conduce to prosperity a *specific* appreciation for the nuances of a particular culture that constitute its own way to foster an enterprising spirit.

Take the reforming soviet-type economies as a case in point. First of all the institutional policies of traditional soviet-type systems are clearly crucial explanatory factors in assessing their poor performance. The *main* difference between, say, South and North Korea, or between the Western and the Eastern parts of Germany, or between Hong Kong or Taiwan and mainland China, stems from the failed pattern of institutional policies of soviet-type economies. But still, the way communism worked historically in Korea or Germany or China, has been shaped in fundamental ways by the specific cultures in these societies, and the particular paths they will need to take in the future to build working market economies will depend on culture. Indeed, it could be argued that especially now, in the aftermath of the collapse of orthodox communism, the question of economic culture is crucial. So long as we faced stark policy choices in terms of communism versus capitalism, the divergent institutional patterns of these systems could dominate over the issue of culture, but now, when nearly the whole world is trying to make market systems work better, the cultural underpinnings of economic institutions have gained a new importance.

If only the universal characteristics of markets were relevant in assessing the prospects for a successful reform process, then we would expect that the removal of restrictive laws banning trade in formerly soviet economies would automatically inspire a flood of entrepreneurial activity. The inefficiencies of the former system would quickly be swept away. In some cases there has not been enough privatization of property to lead economists to have expected much economic improvement anyway, but in many Eastern European countries the institutional changes have been rather substantial and it would seem should have yielded more significant results. Without taking cultural factors into account, we are unable to explain why the reforms have not inspired a swift return to market coordination and a rapid charge towards prosperity. Only when we take notice of the cultural shifts which took place during the soviet experiment can we understand the difficulties facing economic recovery today. For example, within the soviet-type economy, affluence was broadly recognized as a sign of being politically advantaged within a totalitarian system, so naturally the wealthy do not tend to inspire much trust. The derogatory term "New Russians" is applied equally to those who have earned their wealth through legitimate business ventures as it is to those who have used Mafioso tactics. Transforming this attitude will be crucial if the business community is to achieve legitimacy in the eyes of ex-soviet citizens.

Further, these recommendations must be appropriate to the specific context. We may point to the East Asian dragons as the shining examples of what a high savings rate can do for an economy, but this may be inappropriate to the former soviet situation. Appeals to these citizens to increase the national savings rate fell upon deaf ears. Or more precisely, the appeals cannot be heard over the sound of the television sets, stereos, dishwashers, and countless other items so long denied to the average soviet citizen. Rather than generalizing a model from a specific context in the East Asian experience, we ought to be identifying the potential sources of growth within the former soviet context. For example, entrepreneurial talent was often exhibited in dealings within the black market. Even more often, meeting one's goals meant traversing mountains of bureaucracy, and coordinating complex deals of favor swapping. Such skills are sometimes translated into organized crime, but they may also be translated into certain forms of commerce. Perhaps the ex-soviet skill at deal making and power brokering can make for market niches in negotiating with foreign business groups. Successful entrepreneurs will be those who identify, either consciously or tacitly, the particular cultural resources the economies possess to foster new opportunities. Successful policy will, in part, depend upon whether the cultural resources are available to support the given policy.

4.2 For example, different kinds of entrepreneurship

Identifying the comparative cultural advantages of a society involves the kind of intimate familiarity with the culture that ethnography can achieve. This means we may need to forsake the grand account that sums up all the world's cultures in a single book, but it may bring us to some useful specifics about how market and cultural processes actually work.

For the purposes of this study, culture is a society's collection of meanings which emerges through social interaction, and which allows the individual to interpret her own circumstances. This interpretive process results in patterns of behavior across individuals that we call cultural structures. We will be arguing that important cultural structures underlie each of the institutional and policy factors driving economic development which economists properly emphasize, so that a better grasp of a particular culture would greatly enhance our understanding of its economic processes.

4.2.1   Entrepreneurship in its context

The kind of theoretical reconciliation between individualist and communalist anthropologies that Albrecht Wellmer proposed (as discussed in the previous chapter) has its counterpart in the empirical diversity of the communal or individual tendencies one finds across cultures. He says that the individualists had a point about negative freedoms. A protected domain of individual rights, including property rights, civil liberties, religious freedom, and so forth, is *necessary* to a free and democratic society, as argue the individualists.

But *not sufficient*, as argue communalists. It is not enough merely for each person to enjoy a protected sphere of liberty. A free democratic society requires a public space, a forum of public discourse about our common concerns, our mutual rights and responsibilities, whether it takes the form of the agora of Greek democracy, or the traditional New England town meeting, or some sort of hypertextual discourse over the Internet, or some other forum. Moreover, one might add, markets and business organizations require their own public spaces, and are, for most human societies, key elements of communal life. For markets to work it is not enough that individuals are protected from attack by one another; there needs to be a shared culture of respect for certain contractual and property rights, and some sort of forum – such as a common law court system – at which to deliberate about just what our rights are, to adjudicate among parties in conflict, and to articulate common principles and standards of conduct.

The variety of the mix between individualism and communalism that one finds in different cultures – between highly individualistic market exchange to communal structures on a rich variety of corporate, caste, kinship, or other bases – is rather wide. But there is no purely atomistic individualist culture; nor is there a purely communal society. No matter how "individualistic" a maverick American entrepreneur may appear to observers from other cultures, none is an island. There are always credit, customer/supplier, and information sharing networks that link entrepreneurs into regularized patterns of exchange. In short, all production is team production, and thus by its very nature, production is social. On the other hand, no matter how communally focussed some cultures may appear to us, one can usually find underneath a fundamental, perhaps even somewhat principled respect for the autonomy of individuals. Working societies find their own balance – just how independent, or how interconnected in various dependent networks, entrepreneurs are – that works in their context (see Landa 1991).

Consider, for example, the relative success of direct selling organizations, such as Amway and Mary Kay Cosmetics, in three distinct settings: the United States, Taiwan, and Japan. Such organizations are based on two key principles: individualism and community. Success is gained primarily through individual initiative, but this is supported with community recognition of individual effort. This support is sometimes in the form of ritual through award ceremonies, is sometimes tangible in the awarding of company vehicles, and is always structural as the hierarchical commission schedule encourages peer monitoring.

Nicole Biggart (1990) argues that the reasons for the success of direct selling organizations differ from one culture to another. The emphasis on individual effort fits in well with the American work ethic, but the emphasis on community has been a particular draw for American women. Often inexperienced in business and suffering from a lack of confidence in commerce, many American women find the direct selling organizations a nurturing (rather than invasive) environment to seek personal as well as financial growth. Taiwanese direct selling organizations excel in the recruitment of family members to join the organization while at the same time advancing their own status in the hierarchy. Given American attitudes against nepotism, this has not been a significant part of U.S. experience. Taiwanese direct selling organizations allow the entrepreneur to operate more like a sole proprietor than working for a more traditional business. This aspect of the direct selling organization tends to be emphasized far less in Japan, where loyalty to the corporation is stressed. Each society draws upon a different set of cultural tools to make the most of this particular form of direct marketing.

Similar cultural patterns conducive to economic growth may emerge from vastly different sources. For example, while Weber's Calvinist ethic of hard work came from the doctrine of predestination, the ethic of hard work among the industrious class of Quakers in the eighteenth and nineteenth centuries emerged from their conviction that salvation occurred through the good works done here on earth.

The spirit of enterprise comes in many different flavors. Each culture creates a unique entrepreneurial pattern; each culture articulates its own genre of stories in which economic leaders achieve wealth-generating success within the specific institutional and customary contours of the society in which they live. Appreciating the rich diversity of these narratives requires many of the skills that the discipline of cultural studies fosters. For example, different societies establish different rules for acquiring credit and different routes for entree into the business world. (See Kotkin 1992 for an analysis of how some ethnic groups have established international networks which capitalize on culturally specific characteristics.)

Consider the distinct cases of the Japanese and the overseas Chinese entrepreneur. In either case, the entrepreneur performs the vital functions of innovation and coordination within the market. Yet in each case, the ideal type or quintessential entrepreneur would be described as having quite different qualities. This is because the role of the entrepreneur in each society originates from fundamentally different sources. The typical entrepreneur will reflect the specific cultural context out of which he or she emerges. The process of acquiring credit, accumulating capital, and getting started in business will also reflect this specific context. The primary source of capital may be the extended family, trade organizations, or formal banking institutions. The rules which operate under each set of circumstances will support some kinds of entrepreneurship, while inhibiting others. Thus, the framework within which this ideal typical entrepreneur must operate will set out both opportunities and limits.

In Western and Chinese cultures we often think of entrepreneurs as mavericks, yet the standard account of Japanese business culture is centered around team and group identity. The ideal-typical Japanese entrepreneur fits into an already existing structure of authority and power. Within the firm, corporate unity is held in high regard, while individual identity is subordinated to that of the corporation. Employment within the corporation can even supersede kinship connections in terms of loyalty and priority. Though the ideal of life-long employment within the company has come under tremendous pressure over the past decade, tight bonds of firm loyalty are still characteristic of Japanese corporate culture. Firms converge into higher and higher levels of vertical and horizontal integration. Through mergers and layers upon layers of subcontracting agreements, firms assemble themselves into large corporate groups, referred to as "enterprise group capitalism." Once firms begin the process of aligning themselves into corporate groups, other competing firms must follow suit or perish (Tam 1990). The result is a remarkable stability both within the firm and among firms.

Though the thesis has been criticized, many have argued that this model for industrial organization has emerged as a result of Confucian ethics. As described by Herman Kahn as early as 1979, the Confucian tradition of Chun-tzu, or the principal concern for duty and propriety, is responsible for the work ethic found in Japanese society (Kahn 1979). It is argued that out of this philosophical system emerged a strong ethic towards a stringent meritocracy, but one within the context of an exacting hierarchy. Thus, there is a balance being struck between individual achievement, and the eventual subordination of the purposes of the individual to the larger goal of the collective.

Others have challenged this thesis on the role of the Confucian ethic. Murakami (1986) argues that the Confucian ethos is not the primary cultural force at play, but rather that the Samurai military organization has had the greatest influence on corporate culture in Japan. The subordination of kinship ties to corporate ties relates to the functional role of membership within the military organization (Clegg and Redding 1990). Placement within the hierarchy of the corporation is not primarily a consequence of class, but on the contrary there is the opportunity for upward (as well as downward) mobility within the same firm. Murakami suggests that this is the modern manifestation of cultural structures adopted within the Samurai era where not one's class but one's function within the hierarchy was what defined status. This functional role of membership had the advantage of inspiring individual effort in hopes of upward mobility, but this was mobility within the confines of a stable authority. In much the same way, the modern Japanese firm inspires individual effort and peer competitiveness, but within the framework of the corporation, which offers a level of authority that transcends individual ambition in relative importance.

Japanese training practices involve not only the technical expertise needed to accomplish the job, but the socialization of the employee into the corporate culture as well. Training is highly firm specific. Positions within one company are not usually seen as stepping stones to other firms or industries. The hope (if not expectation) on the part of both the employer and employee is a career-long commitment. This has a moral dimension, much like the life-long commitment people may have to their family. The effect has been a lack of mobility across the market for most Japanese workers. They tend not to seek employment with competitors, nor are they likely to be sought. The high degree of job security one has does not mean that status within the hierarchy is guaranteed, however, again allowing for innovation as the result of individual effort and ambition, but at the same time subordinating the goals of the individual employee to that of the corporate authority. This appeal to authority stems from traditional beliefs concerning the family. Munkata (1988) argues that corporate employees identify with the corporation, as individuals once identified with the family or village community. Munkata (1988: 174) observes:

> In industrial enterprises, the role of managers is important for integrating the organizations, which is done by the enterprise as a culturally meaningful system to newly "adopted" employees. The managers usually set up well-prepared in-house educational programs, some of which include intensive training in foreign languages or even in the practice of contemplation in Zen temples.

4.2.2   Culture versus rationality?

Stewart Clegg and S. Gordon Redding (1990) challenge theses such as these which place culture at the forefront of analysis when explaining Japanese economic growth. They argue that culture is not the source of Japanese success. Rather, the success has come from performance measures such as quality control and segmentary work practices where corporate firms train their employees in such a manner that their skills will be firm specific, and therefore of little use to a competing firm. Clegg and Redding contend that these measures are not the product of Post-Confucian or Samurai military culture, but rather simply savvy corporate management at work. To the extent that these practices have any cultural component (such as morning ceremonies or group exercise), they argue that it is the calculated choice of management to use these symbols of culture. Traditional symbolism and ceremonies, they argue, are mere "decorative additions" and have no real consequence. Thus, the adoption of these rules of conduct, and the use of traditional rules of authority and hierarchy are the result of an attempt to maximize profits, not a reflection of deep-seated cultural responses. To reinforce this argument, Clegg and Redding cite Berger and Luckmann (1966) who caution that "the social construction of reality should never be regarded as a disinterested affair." In short, they argue that culture has little to do with Japanese growth. Profit motive is the only explanation needed.

The essential problem with this argument is that it understands cultural influences to be a counter-rational force; it says that if one is under the influence of culture one must not be "acting rationally." Further, it misunderstands economic decisions to be "purely" calculating and atomistic, i.e., having nothing at all to do with culture. On the first point, clearly an individual does not wholly choose his culture as he would choose an item in the grocery store. The individual inherits a language community, values, and ethics. On the other hand, this does not mean that cultural influences lie outside of rationality. While we do not choose the cultural influences which shape our perspective, we have it within our grasp to challenge inherited cultural norms. While an individual cannot wholly transform his cultural perspective, he can choose to broaden it, to amend it, and perhaps most important to the discussion at hand, to *use it*. Berger and Luckmann's counsel was aimed directly to this point.

Not only should we not completely divorce culture from rationality, we make a similar mistake if we see decisions concerning profit, the epitome of rational choice, as lying outside the influence of culture. All profit-making decisions take place within a specific cultural context. What constitutes a wise economic decision will depend upon the cultural context in which it is made. Entrepreneurship is not calculation. Wise entrepreneurial decisions do not come algorithmically. As Lavoie has argued elsewhere, entrepreneurship is an interpretive process, requiring that the interpretation come from a specific perspective.

> Profit opportunities are not so much like road signs to which we assign an automatic meaning as they are like difficult texts in need of a sustained effort of interpretation. Entrepreneurship is not only a matter of opening one's eyes, of switching on one's attentiveness; it requires directing one's gaze. When an entrepreneur sees things others have overlooked, it is not just that he opened his eyes while others had theirs closed. He is reading select aspects of a complex situation others have not read. And this raises the question of what gives a pre-directedness to the entrepreneur's vision, of why he is apt to read some things and not others. (Lavoie 1991: 46)

We think that one of the main things that directs the entrepreneur's vision is culture. Entrepreneurial decision-making is not some sort of pure calculation but a complex reading of the polysemic dialogue of the market. It is necessarily embedded within a cultural context. In most cases, however, exactly how culture shapes entrepreneurial perspective is not a process that can be explicitly specified. Entrepreneurs may not be aware of how their own focus is directed by the cultural context in which they operate. In fact, it is usually when the cultural context is unfamiliar that entrepreneurs are likely to pay closer attention to it. Learning how to "read" any particular cultural context – learning to discern profit opportunities, for example – is a process which makes use of tacit or inarticulate knowledge. Friedrich Hayek made this point about economic knowledge. Certainly, any entrepreneurial decision will employ explicit data such as the prices of inputs and demographic statistics. But Hayek pointed out that entrepreneurs also make use of inarticulate knowledge, perhaps derived from the experience of many years within a particular industry, which enables them to make sense of all the many bits of information available to them. Similarly, one might be able to explicitly define a list of cultural rules they wish to employ in securing greater productivity, such as in the case of the Japanese managers. But "cultural knowledge" is not just a list of rules one holds inside one's head. Rather, culture provides a framework of meaning that allows entrepreneurs to make sense of all the various, often conflicting pieces of information. Culture gives shape to the interpretive process that is entrepreneurship.

It may indeed be the case that Japanese managers are making a conscious choice to use traditional rules of authority and hierarchy when training their employees. The possibility that they are, however, does not undermine the thesis that the cultural influences at play in society are important in explaining economic performance. In this case, the crucial question is not what is motivating the manager, but rather, why does this particular strategy work?

4.2.3 Cultural fit

As a way of making the argument that cultural symbolism, ceremony, and training techniques are mere window dressing, Clegg and Redding point to the fact that in many of the overseas Japanese firms, in Singapore for example, management has chosen to drop these elements of Japanese culture. In other countries such as the U.S., where the practices were not abandoned, "Difficulties [were] experienced... Personnel and labor management, often cited as the cultural locus of the organizational expression of 'Post-Confucianism', [were] in fact, the weak points of Japanese management overseas" (Clegg and Redding 1990: 46). American employees often find morning exercise rituals to be paternalistic and presentations designed to instill a "team-spiritedness" to be forced camaraderie.

Yet, rather than proving the "culture as window dressing" thesis, this speaks directly to the importance such cultural influences play in the economic sphere. If the elements of Japanese culture used in management were simply window dressing, then there should have been no differences when they were transported abroad. The fact that they were a weak point in overseas management suggests that these practices "fit" in one context, but not in another. We should not be surprised by the fact that practices which seem paternalistic and invasive (in one context) will lead to lower productivity. Yet, this also suggests that these same practices might yield positive results if they reflect and accommodate the particular cultural context elsewhere.

Again, consider the differences among the Japanese emphasis upon hierarchy and the Chinese emphasis on sole proprietorship. One would normally expect that strong traditions of mutual trust would be a necessary condition for the effective development of markets. (See for example, Fukuyama 1995.) As Tam points out, there is something to be explained here. The overseas Chinese economic success flies in the face of much conventional wisdom. Relating the Hong Kong experience, Tam (1990: 153) reports:

> ... widespread disloyalty and lack of commitment of employees to companies, pervasive neglect of human resource development within companies, extremely limited trust and openness between employers and employees, constant disintegration of firms into units of atomistic size, thereby sacrificing the economies of scale. And yet despite these anomalies Hong Kong has a highly effective work force, an abundant supply of first class entrepreneurs and businessmen, constant renewal of firms and gigantic industrial power.

Similar accounts could be given for South Korea, Taiwan, Singapore, as well as the many immigrant Chinese communities in the United States, the U.K., and Canada (see Kotkin 1992: 165–200 and Sowell 1983: 21–49). To the extent that overseas Chinese workers stay within the same firm, it tends to be a family business. Firms owned by non-relatives tend to split apart rapidly. The Chinese firm is seen as belonging to the family. Thus, hiring kin into the business is seen as a virtue, not nepotism (Acton 1990). As is the custom with family property, the firm is often divided among family members equally, leading to an inherent decentralization even when the firm is owned by a single family (Tam 1990). While one may enter the business world by working for another firm, only family can expect to advance in the hierarchy, as there exists a pervasive lack of trust for anyone except close relations. Success is seen as ownership; making the jump from employee to employer. Since the chance for a non-relative to achieve ownership of a firm for which he works is virtually nil, the employee eventually leaves the firm, ultimately in pursuit of sole proprietorship.

Given the common experiences of success, the differences among Japanese and overseas Chinese firms are staggering. Whereas Japanese firms foster a life-long sense of stability among workers, Chinese workers are beset with a pervading insecurity. However, both contexts manage to generate a remarkable work ethic.

> The Japanese work hard for their family, as which they see the firm. . . In a secure context the Japanese employee has learned to depend on the company. In an insecure context the Chinese employee has learned to be

self-reliant. In many ways the Chinese are motivated to work in the company but not for the company. (Tam 1990: 177)

Thus while interfirm mobility is highly unlikely in the Japanese context, it is the rule within the overseas Chinese context. The ideal typical Chinese entrepreneur is one who learns by doing. Even with the direct links between kinship and business, most entrepreneurs do not go through an extended apprenticeship. They build their skills through practice, rather than indoctrination.

Alongside the deeply rooted Chinese respect for family is a maverick individualist spirit. The question arises as to why this has emerged as a pervasive influence in the overseas Chinese communities, yet not Japanese society. One reason might be the particular political climate. In Hong Kong, for example, the decades leading up to the return of the province to China may have inspired a single-minded pursuit towards market prosperity (Fong 1988). While this has no doubt had an influence on the operative time horizon among Hong Kong's entrepreneurs, and the energy with which many have pursued their fortune, a similar explanation is lacking for Singapore, Taiwan and South Korea. Another possible explanation for the unique form of East Asian individualism is the influence that Buddhism and folk religions or Shamanism have had. As Berger and Hsiao (1988: 8) suggest:

It is possible to make the argument that, as Buddhism crossed the Tibetan plateau and the great Himalayan passes, it underwent a profound transformation, changing from what was perhaps the most world-denying religion in human history to an emphatically world-affirming one... [Thus, it was in] East Asia that salvation was located consistently in this world.

They go on to say that ultimately it was neither Confucianism nor Buddhism which gave rise to the "in-this-worldliness" but rather the more deeply rooted, highly pragmatic folk religions.

The important point to be made here is that the model for entrepreneurship which operates within the overseas Chinese setting works because it emerges out of that specific context. The Japanese model for the entrepreneur and the firm works because the cultural context supports this ideal. The pessimistic view of this situation would be that since there is no generalizable model for economic development, there is little hope for African, Latin American, or reforming soviet-type countries. Given the cultural specificity of the successful experiences of East Asian countries, there is little chance of mimicking that performance.

The optimistic view, on the other hand, is that with an appreciation for the role culture plays in economic processes, we are in a far better position to identify appropriate courses of action. This does not mean that we should attempt to import cultural systems. Forcing African school children to read

Confucius in hopes of creating an Asian work ethic will be about as successful as requiring middle-aged American factory workers to do morning group calisthenics. What is possible, however, is to identify what cultural advantages are at work within a particular society so as to tap into their potential.

4.2.4   *Cultural studies and public policy*

And then there is the question of "So what?" Say we establish that culture is important in gauging potential economic performance, is there anything we can do about culture? Is it possible to change culture for the better, such that we manage to promote whatever we mean by economic progress? Some discussions of culture and the economy suggest that the more powerful an influence culture is found to be, the less hope there is for us to develop policy measures that can improve the economy. If the economic success of East Asian societies is due simply to judicious trade, fiscal, and monetary policies, then these policies are likely to foster similar results no matter what the context. Yet, if the economic success of East Asian societies is due to Confucian philosophy, Chinese social institutions, habits and customs, then our chances of detecting a generalized model to be transported elsewhere are dim.

Many developing countries (as well as many Western countries) seek to mimic the economic performance experienced by East Asian countries such as South Korea, Taiwan, Hong Kong, Singapore, and Japan. If the "Asian miracle" is due to growth-friendly institutions and policies, it is argued, then we can embrace such institutions and policies here, but if it is due to "Asian values," then there is nothing we can do. We can try to mimic tax policy but we cannot wholly transport cultural value systems from one place to another. Berger and Hsiao (1988: 9) offer two possibilities.

> The answer to the question will hinge to a considerable degree on the role one will eventually ascribe to cultural factors in the economic performance of the region. Broadly speaking, two hypotheses are possible here, one "culturalist," the other "institutionalist." ... If the "institutionalists" are right, there is indeed a model to be exported; if the "culturalists" are right, one must be skeptical of such exportability.

What their argument may lead many economists to conclude, though it certainly is not the conclusion they intended to draw from their analysis, is that since the only actionable part of the causal complex influencing economic development is its institutional part, culture, however powerful its influence, can be ignored.

The study of hundreds of years of experience has shown rather conclusively that no matter what the cultural advantages held by a particular society, without the policies of free trade, a reliable legal framework, a stable monetary system, and a functioning system of private property rights, economic success is highly unlikely if not impossible (see Rosenberg and Birdzell 1986; Baechler 1975). In examining the reasons for success in Hong Kong and Singapore, Pang Eng Fong (1988) finds that economic growth was the result of free trade, low tax rates, and minimal levels of state intervention. But we still need to ask what cultural influences are at play in fostering such an institutional setting? Was there, for example, a significant impact on Hong Kong's culture from its years of British colonial rule? Policies are enacted from a specific cultural context. Underlying politics is what is sometimes called the political culture. Thus, even in recognizing the universal importance of certain institutional factors, we are still drawn back to the issue of culture. To be sure, comparative economic studies between North and South Korea, or East and West Germany, in which the cultural contexts are initially similar, also bear out the significance institutional structure plays in economic success, but this does not render the issue of culture irrelevant. As post-communist countries seek to enact reforms, for example, we see that the institutions necessary for economic progress are often met with marked social resistance. In the course of totalitarian rule, cultural norms conducive to the market order are apt to erode and public policy will have to contend with cultural dimensions of reform.

The role of culture in fostering a vigorous economy goes beyond the momentous function of establishing the social institutions upon which markets rely. The way Berger frames the problem is misleading both because he deploys the language of culture as a factor, and because, as he is fond of saying, he does not accept the Ancient Curse theory of culture. Granted, it would be absurd to suppose that one could "pass a law" that American values should be "more Confucian" or something, but this is not to say that the cultural domain is not actionable.

Many institutional maladies are resistant to the top-down, Pass-a-Law mentality, and can only be overcome by a gradual change in attitudes and practices, but this does not mean there is nothing we can do about them. Knowing what elements of a culture contribute to its economic prosperity is important, even if it cannot be directly translated into a bill in the Senate, or a constitutional amendment. Many of us spend a good deal of our lives in a different sort of "policy activity," and perhaps it is this kind of policy work that is more likely to lead to lasting change. We attempt to pass along to our co-workers, our friends, our neighbors, and our children, the values we take to be conducive to the good life. Some of us spend hours in classrooms, clubs, temples, mosques, or churches conveying values to our students or audiences or congregations, whether we explicitly admit that we are doing so or not. Some of us write articles, letters to the editor, e-mail, or books, in which this or that value of our culture is encouraged or discouraged. Coaches of Little League teams and Girl Scout troup leaders who impart a work ethic, a pride in accomplishments, self-esteem, an ability to work with others, are perhaps more important policymakers in the end than legislators are.

Robert Putnam (1993) refers to the norms and networks of civil society that emerge from such activity as "social capital." Social capital contributes to economic prosperity by lowering transactions and transformation costs. In a study of regional governance in Italy, Putnam *et al.* (1983) found that successful economic performance was correlated with high levels of social capital. Putnam (1993: 37) observes that

> ...[t]hese communities did not become civic simply because they were rich. The historical record strongly suggests precisely the opposite: They have become rich because they were civic. The social capital embodied in norms and networks of civic engagement seems to be a precondition for economic development, as well as for effective government. Development economists take note: Civics matters.

The President of the Czech Republic, Vaclav Havel (1992: 14–15) certainly recognizes that civic culture matters.

> I consider it immensely important that we concern ourselves with culture not just as one among many human activities, but in the broadest sense – the "culture of everything," the general level of public manners. By that I mean chiefly the kind of relations that exist among people, between the powerful and the weak, the healthy and the sick, the young and the elderly, adults and children, business people and customers, men and women, teachers and students, officers and soldiers, policemen and citizens, and so on. . . [H]owever important it may be to get our economy back on its feet, it is far from being the only task facing us. It is no less important to do everything possible to improve the general cultural level of everyday life. . . I would go even farther, and say that, in many respects, improving the civility of everyday life can accelerate economic development. . .

Policy analysts and policy makers usually take only institutional factors, not cultural factors into consideration when developing economic policy. The reasons for this most likely lie in one of two perspectives: they either think that culture is of little or no consequence, or that while it is possible to dictate institutional policy measures, it is impossible to dictate culture. To the first point, we have already offered a detailed response, that indeed cultural processes play a crucial role in defining the economic course a society will take. To the second point, we recognize the questionableness of asking government to dictate cultural values. Most economic analysts do not see it as their role to "preach" a certain set of moral or ethical values, even if by following the prescribed values society would have a better chance of enriching itself.

But we must recognize that in endorsing institutional policies, by necessity, we endorse cultural values as well. Consider the cultural shift being endorsed by proposing a "Work to Welfare" reform, or the abandonment of tax-financed transfer payments altogether. Think of the cultural changes we are recommending when we tell reforming soviet-type systems that they need to establish private ownership and allow free trade. Thus, in advocating one or another institutional policy, we are also advocating a specific set of cultural values which go along with that policy. To suggest that policy makers ought to stay out of the business of cultivating values is to misunderstand the nature of values. Public policy can not help but be value laden.

The hesitation to advocate cultural values as a deliberate political policy is understandable. Such preaching conjures up images of social engineering, or ethnocentric chauvinism of the kind Lawrence Harrison exhibits. If a kind of policy activism in regard to culture is possible, it needs to be tempered with a profound sense of respect for existing cultural beliefs. In the age of rationalist constructivism, of aspirations to engineer society's values, we have seen attempts to indict entire systems of social institutions as illegitimate, as Marxism and fascism did in taking to task the "bourgeois institutions" of family, private ownership, and religion. The intricate interrelationships among cultural values and economic institutions should remind us that any attempt to make wholesale changes to culture puts us in danger of losing the valued functions these institutions perform. The greatest social, political, and economic progress has come not from rebuilding social institutions from the ground up, but from evolving incremental changes to our values and practices from within the existing social structure. Change generally occurs gradually and on the margin, where individual norms are questioned and challenged one at a time, still from within the cultural framework, and with the preponderance of the evolved social institutions firmly intact.

Not only are efforts at social engineering or sweeping criticisms of whole cultures repugnant, it is ludicrous to suppose that anybody has the ability to act on these attitudes, to successfully engineer values from on high, or to change a whole society's values. Clearly, the political apparatus can have a major effect on the prevailing culture, but it is an entirely different question as to whether a political apparatus can engineer a culture so as to bring about positive results. The ability to influence and the ability to control are radically different prospects. Surely, we do not want politicians (or academics for that matter) trying to dictate what our culture should be.

But we have argued in Section 2.4 that there is a broader notion of "politics" or of "public policy" that takes neither to mean only how we try to get government to behave. In much of the cultural studies literature the site of politics has shifted, so that we are concerned instead with how we interact with one another in the politics of everyday life, in all our forms of community. What we are suggesting is that the question of culture needs to come into the forefront of public discussion; to include not only academics, but business people, media, parents, even politicians. The point is to recognize that culture plays an important role in both our social as well as economic lives. By identifying the developmentally relevant cultural resources that are operative within different contexts, we will be in a far better position to make policy recommendations for not only developing and reforming economies, but our own as well.

After all, it is always possible for some members of society to influence their culture profoundly. Historically the most influential avenue for the shaping of values has been through "popular culture," the stories, poetry, theatre, and so forth by which fundamental values are imparted. A novel by a Russian revolutionary energized Lenin and led to the Bolshevik experiment, with all its attendant horrors. In our time, movies and television shape the attitudes of millions of citizens in ways that may be seen to be development-resistant or development-promoting. The next chapter takes up this issue.

5 The culture industry's representation of business

There is, on prime time television, a unified picture of life in these United States that is an alternative reality. . . Television land is a world in which the respectable pillars of society turn their daughters out to become prostitutes and heirs kill their mistresses. Businessmen make their real money by turning sweet-faced youngsters into junkies and barely pubescent girls into hookers. . . The world of television is peopled by killers wearing three-piece suits, heroin pushers operating behind a facade of civic responsibility, murderers of go-go dancers sitting behind massive mahogany desks in the corridors of power.

Ben Stein (1980: 87, 105, 203; quoted in Lichter *et al.* 1991: 17)

The previous chapter discussed the way cultural patterns underlie different modes of entrepreneurship, and many of the ways in which entrepreneurial activity can fuel economic development. The American economy is certainly one that has historically reaped enormous benefits from a relatively open entrepreneurial atmosphere, and a culture that has celebrated the enterprising spirit. Yet not all of U.S. society's cultural attitudes celebrate the entrepreneur. In fact, many aspects of popular culture are openly hostile to the business world and the people who inhabit it. In this chapter, we would like to explore the ways activities in the market, particularly in the culture industry, shape and redefine the entrepreneurial values which have traditionally supported the market process.

As the opening quote from Ben Stein suggests, to say that the culture industry's portrayal of business people is unflattering would be a severe understatement. While conservative cultural critics like Stein (1980) have complained about the pervasive negative portrayals of business people in film and on television, for the most part, economists have remained silent on this issue. We suspect that this silence is not so much due to disinterest, as it is to the fact that economists lack the tools of analysis by which we might address the dynamics surrounding the portrayal of business people within popular culture. Yet, addressing and understanding these dynamics is exactly what cultural studies does best.

At the center of cultural studies work is the attempt to understand how messages within popular culture play into people's everyday lives – their choices, attitudes, judgments, and perceptions. For example, Geraghty (1991) and Modleski (1984) demonstrate how fan gossip about soap opera characters provides a sort of "social cement" that binds viewers to the narrative and to each other. Hobson's (1982) and Warth's (1994) ethnographic research of soap opera audiences detail the ways in which television structures viewers' daily routine. Radway's (1984) research on women readers of romance novels illustrates the diverse ways in which texts can be interpreted. She found, for instance, that some women readers increased their assertiveness as a consequence of reading romance novels, even though the female characters were rarely depicted as assertive. Cultural studies goes beyond textual analysis as such. It requires that we understand how people actually receive and reinterpret the messages contained within them. Though to date little work has been done by cultural studies scholars on the portrayal of business people in popular culture, the field certainly possesses the tools to take on the task. In this chapter, we hope to take the preliminary steps needed to undertake this sort of ethnographic research (Moores 1993).

In doing so, we hope to reveal two things. First, to economists we hope to reveal how cultural studies provides a model for how social analysis can benefit by moving beyond the a-cultural non-interpreting agent as the unit of analysis. Cultural studies takes as its starting point human beings who are both embedded within a thick cultural context and who are creative in their responses to that context. We contend that economics has much to learn from cultural studies in this respect. Second, to cultural studies theorists we hope to reveal the world of business and the cultural messages that surround it as an arena which is worthy of their attention. Critiques informed by cultural studies have had tremendous success in uncovering the underlying dynamics at work within popular culture – such as racism, sexism, classism, and homophobia. Not only have they uncovered the underlying messages pitched by writers and producers, they have also uncovered the attitudes among the viewing public which are complicit in their continuation and acceptance. We contend that we have much to learn if we focus that same lens on the portrayal of business people and the business world in the popular media.

We consider this to be an important undertaking in part because we are mindful of the influence cultural attitudes have in shaping economic processes and political policies. If our earlier argument that culture provides the foundational support for economic coordination and progress is correct, then an examination of popular cultural attitudes towards business will be an important part of assessing the health of our economic culture and the prospects for future economic progress. Here, we focus on television and film, but this sort of analysis could certainly be extended to how business people are portrayed in literature, in news analysis, in family stories, and in educational settings. The point is that wherever stories get told about business, new cultural meanings are being constructed. The question is whether the cultural norms that emerge from this process will support or undermine an entrepreneurial culture.

5.1   The image of business in popular culture

The culture industry, in particular the television and film entertainment industry, is itself a major force in American business. Advertising revenue to network, local and cable television companies generates approximately $44.5 billion annually. The average American home has 2.3 television sets, and the average American watches 1,567 hours of television per year, or about 4.3 hours per day. Total annual receipts from the motion picture industry are approximately $60.2 billion, including production and distribution, box office receipts, and video tape rental (US Department of Commerce 1998). On average, American teenagers go to the movies at least once a month, and the average VCR owner rents six video tapes per month (Pampel 1994: 48–9). The American film industry is also an important export industry, dominating almost all of the European film markets and much of the developing world (US Department of Commerce 1998).

Not only do television and cinema play a major financial role in the American economy, they also exert a formidable influence upon American culture. As the popular culture movement in cultural studies shows, it is in this realm of commercial culture where fundamental values are forged. On average, Americans watch more than four hours of television each day. "Even a more conservative estimate of 3 hours means that television absorbs 40 percent of the average American's free time. . ." (Putnam 1996: 46). The average household has at least one television set on at least seven hours a day (Lichter *et al.* 1991: 3). This is not to suggest that having the television turned on is tantamount to Hollywood mind control, but producers and scriptwriters do represent a formidable influence in the dominant culture.

As we argued in Chapter 3, cultural studies has put some distance between itself and the traditional Frankfurt School approach to the culture industry. It challenges the portrayal of the consuming public as a group of mindless victims, passively accepting whatever message the captains of the culture industry invent. In *Television Culture*, John Fiske (1989: 64) describes the move cultural studies has made in this regard.

> Textual studies of television now have to stop treating it as a closed text, that is, as one where the dominant ideology exerts considerable, if not total, influence over its ideological structure and therefore over its reader. Analysis has to pay less attention to the textual strategies of preference or closure and more to the gaps and spaces that open television up to meanings not preferred by the textual structure, but that result from the social experience of the reader.

While cultural studies theorists recognize the potential power of messages received through popular culture, they also recognize the possibility for resistance by the consuming public. Audiences have the potential to "poach" the meaning of texts to serve their own interests (see Hall [1973] 1980; Eco

1972; de Certeau 1984). Once we recognize the agency of the viewing public to resist the messages received through popular culture, their status as passive dupes of the culture industry appears much more problematic.

We will argue that the messages conveyed in popular culture do not on the whole support the legitimacy of business, rather the majority of such messages perpetuate negative stereotypical images of the businessperson, and indict market activity as inherently base and sinister. Yet, we must also recognize that viewers have the potential to resist and reshape such messages. We want to explore the ways in which viewers might reshape such messages, how they might resist or fail to resist the meaning that is pitched by the culture industry, and how they might integrate such messages into their understanding of the business world.

Robert Lichter, Linda Lichter, and Stanley Rothman (1991) surveyed three decades of prime-time television programs to chronicle the alternative reality that is television. The study records racial and sexual trends, the portrayal of law enforcement, home life and the world of work from the 1950s to the 1980s. Not surprisingly, the study finds that the world of television does not usually match up to reality. Television is, after all, fantasy. If drama and intrigue were rationed out on television at the rate they are rationed out in real life, there would not be much point to tuning in. Thus, it is not surprising that the bad guys we meet in televisionland are utterly despicable and that the good characters would be candidates for sainthood if only they were real people. What is surprising, however, are the demographics of the televisionland population, particularly when it comes to crime, adultery, cheating, and other reprehensible behavior. Of all the antagonists studied in over 30 years of programming, businessmen were twice as likely to play the role of antagonist than any other identifiable occupation. Business characters are nearly three times as likely to be criminals, relative to other occupations on television (Lichter *et al.*, 1991: 131). They represent 12 percent of all characters in identifiable occupations, but account for 32 percent of crimes. Forty-four percent of all vice crimes such as prostitution and drug trafficking committed on television, and 40 percent of TV murders, are perpetrated by business people (Lichter *et al.* 1991: 132).

The negative portrayal of business people on television has evolved over the years. In the late 1950s and early 1960s, business people were three times as likely to exhibit characteristics of rampant greed, relative to other characters with identifiable occupations. In the 1980s, business characters were ten times more likely to exhibit greedy behavior relative to other characters (Lichter *et al.* 1991: 144). Yet there has been no similar trend for other occupations.

Prime-time television series in the 1990s seem to have kept pace with this trend. Business people were often portrayed as unscrupulous and tyrannical, as in the case of CBS's *Dr. Quinn, Medicine Woman*. Before its cancellation in 1998, the usual cast of characters included Jake, the bigoted barber and sometimes dentist who spends his spare time roughing up black townspeople and working diligently to keep the vote from women. Hank, the local saloon owner, forces prostitutes into indentured servitude and beats up innocent horses. Lorn, the owner of the general store, demonstrates glimpses of humanity, but more often than not, he sides with Jake and Hank in their immoral causes. The heros of the series are Michaela Quinn, the town doctor who never seems to charge anyone for her services, and the handsome Sully who does not seem to have any occupation save that of Native American rights activist.

Sometimes the anti-business bias leads to defective narratives. Anyone who has been a business person must cringe when JR Ewing tells the person he is bargaining with, as he seemed to in just about every negotiation we saw him make, that he would pay any sum to get what he wanted. This may be some Hollywood writer's idea of a way to show his unscrupulousness, or his enormous wealth, but what it really shows is how innocent of the world of business the writers are. Presumably not too many business persons were in the *Dallas* audience, or at least not many of them cared that the plot was occasionally made so utterly implausible.

Over the last decade, the moral bankruptcy of business characters was evident in films as well. In *Indecent Proposal*, financier John Gage offers a happy but financially strapped couple Diana and David Murphy $1 million for one night with Diana. The pleasure that Gage receives from this indecent proposal is more than just the chance to be intimate with the beautiful Diana. Most of the pleasure he derives comes from the manipulative power he has over their happiness and sense of morality. And it is not only in the invention of fictional stories of business criminality where the bias against businessmen shows up. In the 1996 film *Fargo,* based on a true story, a car salesman has his wife kidnapped so that he can collect the ransom he knows his wealthy father-in-law will pay. Since he is the principal villain in the story, we are not surprised to see the salesman portrayed in a rather negative light, but the producers manage to portray his character more sympathetically than that of the father-in-law, who commits no crimes but whose financial success seems to be the source of a despicable personality.

Lichter *et al.* (1991) did find cases in which wealthy business characters used their fortune to positive ends such as in the series *Hart to Hart* and *Matt Houston.* While we never actually saw them engaged in the business of making money, at least there was some premise for how the wealth was generated. These are the exceptions, however. More often than not, even the premise is absent. Consider the *Star Trek* series and its spin-offs *Star Trek, The Next Generation, Deep Space Nine,* and *Star Trek, Voyager.* The "Federation of Planets" maintains one of the most advanced space exploration and defense systems in the universe. The advanced technology is an obvious sign of enormous wealth, yet there is never any mention of the industry or commerce which one would presume makes Star Fleet possible. Picard, the *Enterprise* captain in *The Next Generation* once arrogantly announced to a twentieth-century cryonics survivor that there is no longer a need for a business mentality in the twenty-fourth century as they have eliminated want. In *The*

Next Generation, we do meet a few business people from "other worlds," but in the end they turn out to be glorified drug dealers or antiquities thieves. Interestingly, *Deep Space Nine* regularly features the "Ferenge," a truly entrepreneurial species. While these characters are somewhat loveable, they are also annoying, not to mention ugly. The Ferenge are driven by an ethic of "greed is good." The only other overriding concern would be their wanton lust, which may stray them temporarily from their pursuit of profits. Ultimately, however, the Ferenge are outsiders to the Star Fleet crew. It is not to the Ferenge or any like them that the Federation owes their existence.

Unbridled greed has provided dramatic theme for centuries. This, combined with the American love of the underdog, might very well render the business person an obvious target of any screenwriter or producer. Yet as Lichter *et al.* (1991) point out, if the overwhelmingly negative image the business person has endured in popular culture were simply the celebration of the "little guy" and an anti-authoritarian sentiment, then big business would receive more severe treatment than small business, since presumably the small shop owner holds no extraordinary power. Yet, in fact, this was not the case. Big business characters fared better than small business operators. Worse yet were salesmen, realtors, and stockbrokers. (Lichter *et al.* 1991: 134). In a follow-up study, Robert Lichter, Linda Lichter, and Daniel Amundson controlled for wealth to test the challenge that it is wealthy people, not business people who are portrayed negatively in television programming. Lichter *et al.* (1997: 68–84) found that:

> Business people were portrayed more negatively than other characters at high, medium, and low levels of income. Far from demonstrating that wealth is stigmatized, these data show that a majority (54%) of rich non-business characters were actually portrayed positively. Even among the wealthy, it was only business people who behaved badly more often than not. . . Business characters at *every* economic level were portrayed more negatively than non-business characters at *any* economic level. Thus, the observed association between wealth and negative portrayals proved spurious.

For example, it is the banker's assistant Carl Bruner in *Ghost* (the top grossing film in 1990), who has the hero Sam Wheat killed in order to access the bank's accounts and launder $4 million for an organized crime syndicate. Again, populism and anti-authoritarianism cannot explain Hollywood's disdain for the business person.

World-wide trends in privatization in the late 1980s and 1990s have produced fresh fodder for screenwriters. Apparently, the private contracting of some social services is enough to bring about widespread urban decay in the near future dystopian world of *Robocop,* first released in 1987. The general moral decline is consequence of the fact that the Omni Consumer Products (OCP) corporation now supplies medical services, space exploration, law enforcement and prison facilities. Dick Jones, Division President of the OCP subsidiary Security Concepts wants to place a security android on the street even though it often makes "mistakes" and kills innocent people. The profits which can be earned from the spare-parts market are enough to placate any guilt Mr. Jones might otherwise have. Further, Jones kills a subordinate who "did not go through proper channels," and regularly conspires with Detroit's most notorious drug lord. By the release of *Robocop 3* in 1993, OCP had not changed for the better. Now they wished to build a new city by first destroying all the homes in Detroit, forcing residents into relocation camps. The reluctant refugees would then be forced to work in the factories of the new Delta City, all owned and operated by OCP. The question of who was going to purchase the products OCP produced after the consumers' assets had all been destroyed was left unanswered. Indeed, the entire scenario makes no sense at all.

Not only are business people in the world of television and film inherently corrupt, but profit itself is also put on trial. According to their updated study, Lichter *et al.* found that "sixty-eight episodes. . . contained a major plot development that turned on the question of whether business dealings were either honest and honorable or unfair, corrupt, or illegal. . . Eighty-one percent of shows coded for this variable portrayed business as dishonest and corrupt" (Lichter *et al.* 1997). Rather than a reward for offering valued goods and services, profit is ordinarily portrayed as the result of exploitation and fraud.

In *Total Recall* (the fifth top money-making film of 1990), Arnold Schwarzenegger's character Douglas Quaid battles despot/monopolist Vilas Cohagen, the only supplier of air to colonists on Mars. Cohagen made his fortune by exploiting mine workers on Mars, providing them with inadequate protection against the elements. The early colonists suffered genetic mutations, while Cohagen made his millions. His principal concern is to maintain control over the supply of air for which he charges successively higher prices. In *The Fugitive* (the third top grossing film in 1993), Dr. Richard Kimble is sentenced to die for the brutal murder of his wife, a murder he did not commit. Upon escaping from prison, he sets out to find his wife's killer and to clear his name. Ultimately he learns that the Devlin Macgregor Pharmaceuticals company had meant to kill Kimble, as he had discovered that "Provasic-RDU 90," a drug developed by Devlin Macgregor, causes liver damage. When Kimble was sentenced to die in the electric chair, their problem was solved, or so they thought. In the top money-making film of 1997 *The Lost World*, capitalist Peter Ludlow puts the entire city of San Diego at risk by bringing dinosaurs back to the United States to start a Jurassic theme park. Even when death, destruction and mayhem ensue, Ludlow can only think about his dream of making millions of dollars. The search for profits in the land of cinema is indeed dirty business.

If business is not used to defraud or exploit people directly, it is used as a front for illegal activity. The top grossing film of 1989 was *Batman*. Most remember Jack Nicholson's portrayal of the ghoulish Joker, yet lest we forget, before he was The Joker, he was Jack Napier, top executive in a conglomerate corporation which owned Axis Chemical Company. The main purpose of the company was to launder proceeds from their lucrative organized crime syndicate. The Joker eventually announces his presence to Gotham City by poisoning cosmetic products with chemicals made at Axis Chemicals. In the 1998 film *Lethal Weapon 4*, villain Benny Chan runs several Chinese restaurants and nightclubs as a front to launder money from his counterfeiting operation and the money he makes from selling illegal Chinese immigrants into indentured servitude.

Now of course you would expect that some stories would be circulated in American culture in which the bad guys are all business executives. What you might not expect is that there are hardly any stories in which the good guys are business executives.

In questioning the images of business in popular culture one risks appearing to be humorless, to be a spoil-sport. After all, watching the exaggerated character of the greedy Ferenge businessman Quark on *Deep Space Nine*, or even more dangerous business villains, is great fun, and in itself seems quite harmless. Surely anybody who takes offense at this should lighten up. We admit that we find much of this utterly enjoyable. The point, though, is that the pattern of ridicule is unbalanced. Anyone who found the 1950s depiction of African-Americans in film and television offensive would have been told to lighten up too. Many Blacks laughed along, but sometimes must have wondered why White characters were not playing the fool a bit more often.

5.2   The construction of meaning

We could try, as some cultural conservatives do, to write this phenomenon off as simply a cultural conspiracy on the part of Hollywood. As Lichter, Stein and others point out, there is a strong leftist bias among the principal decision-makers in Hollywood. Seven out of ten Hollywood producers believe that government intervention is a necessary and desirable way to substantially reduce income disparities among rich and poor. Forty-four percent would favor a government guaranteed jobs program (Lichter *et al*. 1991: 14). Yet, we should not forget that film and television producers are business people too. To intentionally undermine attitudes towards all business would be at least somewhat counter productive. It is also important to remember that as business people, producers produce what they think will sell in the market place. Thus, they must be reading the consumer as desiring such stories. At least these stories, when presented with the requisite amount of drama and excitement, are acceptable in the sense that they do not move the audience to reject the work as flawed or valueless on the basis of the unrealistically anti-business themes which are conveyed.

5.2.1 Reading the texts of popular culture

A peculiar similarity exists between the cultural conservatives on the right, who argue that Hollywood producers systematically indulge their leftist ideology to undermine the free-enterprise system, and critics of popular culture coming from the traditional left, who argue that the culture industry conspires to maintain the dominance of the commercial elite. Both arguments ignore the role played by the viewer. Both sides fail to ask how it is that such cultural messages actually get read by the public. If we are to go beyond the cultural conspiracy theories, we need to do more than document the negative portrayals of business people in popular culture. The cultural studies movement insists that we ask how it is that readers of popular culture actually receive such messages. While we do not intend to fully answer this question here – as such work requires in-depth ethnographic research which lies beyond the scope of the current project – we do want to at least pose the question and explore its implications. How do film patrons and television viewers read, respond to, and ultimately integrate negative images of business people into their daily lives?

The role the reader or audience plays in constructing the meaning of a text has been a central theme in the evolution of cultural studies. Cultural studies theorists came out of a tradition that took texts and their meaning seriously, but audiences traditionally had not been recognized as a potential source of that meaning. What has come to be known as "reception theory" places audiences at the center of how we understand the construction of meaning. Stuart Hall's ([1973] 1980) work represents some of the early steps taken within media research that treated the reader as a full participant in the construction of meaning. Earlier film and media studies had explored the relationship between the text and spectator, but the audience was largely cast in the role of passive recipient, not active participant. Informed mainly by a combination of linguistic theory, psychoanalysis, and Marxism, film and media studies sought to understand what sort of audience was being implied by the text itself, but the analysis "failed to distinguish between the reader implied by or inscribed in the text and the actual social subjects who interpret or decode texts" (Moores 1992: 142).

Hall ([1973] 1980) recognized that a single text might take on a variety of meanings as different groups of people holding different positions in the social structure (as determined by socio-economic class, in particular) interpret the text from their particular perspective. Ethnographic work that built upon Hall's analysis further identified the role different "interpretive communities" played in the construction of meaning. David Morley's (1980) study *The Nationwide Audience* is an early example of how ethnographic research can reveal the ways in which viewers construct meanings that reflect their particular social position and access to social discourse. Morley's work challenged the perspective advanced by MacCabe (1976) and others that the text defined the position of the audience. Instead, he argued that audiences meet the text with partially or fully formed ideological positions and life experience that enable them to negotiate their own position with regard to the text. Similarly, research on soap opera audiences has revealed the gendered nature of interpretive readings (Kreutzner and Warth 1994). Not only does the reader's position within society shape their interpretive reading, so too does the context in which people read such texts. The same person watching the same episode of *The Brady Bunch* might have two very different readings, depending upon whether they are watching it in their living rooms at home or if they are watching it in a classroom as part of a media studies course (Moores 1992). Similarly, watching television programs while caring for children and carrying out domestic chores (Hobson 1982) is quite a different thing from ritually tuning in to a favorite program with like-minded fans who give their undivided attention to the program (Jenkins 1992).

Reception theory casts serious doubt on both the traditional left's position that popular culture manipulates the masses into serving the capitalist machine and the conservative position that Hollywood producers are out to destroy the public's faith in free enterprise. Even if the goal of the Hollywood establishment was to systematically destroy the public trust in business, the meaning that the audience takes away with them when they watch a television program or movie is not fully dictated by the producer or screenwriter. It is important to take into account the complex relationship between the production and the consumption of culture. Audiences interpret what they see from their own specific contexts.

Recognizing the multiplicity of meanings a text might take on is not to favor a mindless relativism in which *any* interpretation is as valid as any other. (Or as Jamie Lee Curtis points out to Kevin Kline in the film *A Fish Called Wanda*, "Aristotle was *not* Belgian. The central message of Buddhism is *not* 'every man for himself.' And the London Underground is *not* a political movement.") Nor are we ignoring the role played by the author or producers in creating the meaning of popular culture texts. As Hall (1980) recognized, in framing the way in which the story gets told, the author constructs some of the "limits and parameters" of the possible interpretations that the reader might take away (Hall 1980: 135). Hall argues that the dominant culture, and its agents, such as screenwriters and producers, will still determine the "preferred meaning" implied within a popular culture text, i.e., the meaning which supports the dominant culture. But the potential for resistant readings and reinterpretations by the audience also exists. The openness of the text allows the reader to bring her own interpretive framework to it, allowing for the possibility that new meaning can be created in the process of reinterpretation.

One of the principal reasons why audiences interpret different meanings from a given text, particularly over time, is that audiences have the potential to create and adopt new frameworks of resistance. In other words, new messages may be drawn from a text as a reader becomes more aware of the underlying social dynamics at work in how a story gets told or how characters are represented. The meaning Bernard Shaw's *Pygmalion* takes on today is different from the meaning it acquired at the turn of the century. As late twentieth-century feminists reread the play, new truth was revealed about the ascriptive roles gender and class play in society.

As this has been true in the literary world, it is true of film and television. In the classic silent film *The Birth of a Nation*, released in 1914, the Ku Klux Klan are portrayed as protectors of decency and feminine virtue, as the sheet-clad cavalry ride in to rescue the White victims of Black hostility. Today we see the film not as a representation of the righteousness of the KKK warrior, as producer and director D. W. Griffith most likely intended, but rather as symbolic of the racial climate of 1914. The point is that the texts take on different meanings, not just because of the passage of time, but because the readers have distinctly different perspectives.

Since 1914, American film audiences have acquired a framework of thought that allows them to question and actively resist the intended racist message. Again, this is not to say that the intended meaning of the producers and screenwriters is not of any consequence, but that the creation of meaning is a collaborative process in which both the author and reader, situated within a specific context, actively participate. Lichter *et al.* (1991) grapple with the chicken and egg question of which influences which: does the audience influence the producers (i.e., market demand for such plot lines is driving the supply) or are Hollywood producers the puppet masters manipulating our perceptions? We propose that this is not an either/or situation. In fact, some of each must be influencing the other. As cultural studies scholars point out, any process of reading involves a creative dialogue between the reader and the text. Producers and screenwriters reflect their own perceptions of the world in their scripts and productions, yet all work presumes an audience. Not only is this true in a commercial sense, that the very reason to produce television and film is to provide entertainment (and therefore space for businesses to advertise) but this is true of art in general. Conveying a message only has meaning if there is someone to whom the message will eventually be conveyed. This presumed audience is the target of the producer's and screenwriter's interpretive process. They must interpret how their potential audience interprets the world, in order to provide not only that which is dramatic and exciting, but that which is plausible as well. The script writers reflect this "interpretation of interpretations" in their plot lines and dialogue.

As Grossberg (1992) argues, the relationship between audience and screenwriters is a discursive one. Though the analogy of a conversation is imperfect – this particular "conversation" being highly diffuse – there is clearly a give and take. The audience responds to a text by directly challenging it, accepting it, or negotiating new meaning out of the overlapping structures of resistance they bring to the text. Understanding these responses, at least to some degree, is essential if the screenwriters and producers are to succeed in persuading audiences to see a film or remain loyal to a television series. Though the response is not as immediate and complete as it might be in a real conversation, the screenwriters and producers do nonetheless respond, both to audience reaction and to the reactions of sponsors. To the extent that the interpretations of producers and screenwriters match up with the perceptions of the audience, the text will tend to reinforce already accepted social norms. The truth claims that are "successful" in this sense will tend to be further reinforced by future plot lines which proved successful in the past. On the other hand, as consumers of popular culture resist or reject the messages they see perpetuated in television and film, again, screenwriters and producers respond. Such responses carve out new truth claims which will be read and interpreted, accepted or resisted by an audience actively engaged in this participatory conversation.

Thus, the culture industry does play a significant role in shaping social values, ethics, and behavioral norms, but the particular content of those cultural values and norms is never fully dictated by one side of the process. The construction of meaning is a dynamic process in which the audience participates, along with the producer and screenwriter. Culture both shapes and is shaped by what is seen on the big and little screens. To argue that the entertainment media of film and television have a dramatic impact on how we perceive the world is not to inflate or exaggerate its influence. Nor is this to argue that the audience is a mere puppet at the mercy of the Hollywood producer's strings. While the producers decide which film and television programs will be promoted in any given season, it is ultimately the audience who decides what will survive in the market, as well as how what survives gets interpreted. Just as an interdependent relationship exists in the market, so too an interdependent relationship exists in the construction of meaning.

5.2.2   *Resistance and susceptibility in the creation of meaning*

The collaborative nature of meaning construction implies an array of possible responses, both by audiences and by authors and producers. That a viewer might adopt a variety of interpretive lenses in order to read a popular culture text is well understood within cultural studies. What is less well understood is how an individual comes to adopt a particular interpretive lens. Hall (1980) argued that socio-economic class is the determining factor in how a popular culture text gets read. If the viewer, say a White middle-class male, operates within the dominant culture, his interpretive lens will tend to reproduce the "preferred meanings" of the dominant culture. A viewer who is socially situated outside of the dominant culture, say a Latino migrant farm worker, possesses an ideological framework which allows him to resist the preferred meaning embedded within the text. Yet most viewers are not positioned in purely dominant or purely opposing roles, and must negotiate the overlapping and often contradictory interpretations they read from a text. "These sorts of negotiated readings are ones produced by ideological cooperative readers who read 'with' the structures of the text and seek to match their social experiences with the ideology-in-the-text" (Fiske 1996:

125). In viewing the program *Ally McBeal*, for instance, a middle-class White woman may read the off-beat behavior of the lead character as a challenge to the professional norms set up by the male establishment, yet accept the dominant cultural message that the character will only be truly happy when she finds a male companion.

Though the social position of the viewer allows for these negotiated meanings, Hall emphasizes that the class structure at work within society tends to reproduce and legitimate the values of the dominant culture. Fiske (1989), on the other hand, argues that Hall places too much emphasis on socio-economic class as the source of resistance to the preferred meanings embedded within a text. Fiske, and others engaged in ethnographic studies of audiences, extend Hall's analysis to include sexual orientation (Schiff 1985), gender (Hobson 1982), membership in a sub-culture, ethnicity (Katz and Liebes 1984), age group, religion, occupation, education, political allegiance, nationality, regionalism, and general life experience, as potential sites of resistant readings. Though admittedly the influence academic perspectives are said to have in society is often inflated, we must not ignore the significant impact the academy can also have in cultivating structures of resistance. Women's Studies, African-American Studies, and Ethnic Studies programs, for instance, have proactively created new structures for resistant readings of the dominant culture.

Yet even as we expand our understanding of the ways in which frameworks of resistance are cultivated, it is clear that complete resistance can never be accomplished. Just as there exists the potential for resistance, a potential susceptibility to messages received through popular culture also exists. All viewers play the messages they receive in popular culture against their own perspective, thereby reinforcing or challenging previously held assumptions and beliefs. A Marxist, for example, will not be "manipulated" into believing that markets can be virtuous and desirable simply by seeing the good works of a small-town banker like George Bailey dramatized in *It's a Wonderful Life*. In fact, the Marxist is likely to conclude that such cultural artifacts are the controlling devices of capitalist society. Likewise, Catholics are not likely to leave the church simply because their favorite priest on *Picket Fences* has a fetish for women's shoes. They are more likely to question the validity of the character rather than reject the church. Similarly, Hodge and Tripp (1986) found that in viewing the American sitcom *Diff'rent Strokes*, Australian Aboriginal children were able to create resistant readings of the text because they had already developed a cultural category that included themselves, Native Americans, and African-Americans. The African-American children and the White adoptive family featured in the program represented to them their relative powerlessness within a White-dominated society. But this particular reading was based on their knowledge of Native American and African-American histories as they related to their own experience. In other words, once a structure of resistance is in place, we are given an interpretive perspective that directs our attention to illegitimate messages and provides us with a language of critique. But without this sort of structure of resistance, the opposing interpretation may not be possible.

Every viewer will hold some principles tenaciously, such that they will not be swayed by cultural images that run to the contrary. Yet no viewer thinks critically on all subjects. There exists a fundamental "susceptibility" whenever a viewer or reader has no critical thought process by which to assess the validity of the claims presented. The educational therapist may be quite critical of media claims to growing cases of learning disabilities among elementary school students, because he is aware of changes in testing procedures which might drive these results. Yet, the biochemist may uncritically accept the media claims on this issue, since she may lack an adequate framework for critical thought on the matter, though on other issues, say, questions of water pollution she may have a better framework for interpretation than the therapist. There is no possibility of disentangling oneself from this state of affairs in totality. In fact, this pervasive susceptibility is reflective of the division of labor and interests that is so important to economic prosperity and the growth of knowledge. It does, however, raise important issues when it comes to the question of how norms regarding the portrayal of business are established.

The meaning the audience attaches to the film *Wall Street*, for example, will depend on the interpretive framework that the viewer brings to the text. A labor activist or an academic Marxist may see this as an honest portrayal of how business works in corporate America. When Gordon Gekko smugly reveals the "truth" that the most powerful people in business produce absolutely nothing, they will likely see this as an accurate assessment of Wall Street trading. A stock broker or an ardent advocate of the market order, on the other hand, will likely resist such messages and reject the implication that blackmail and breaking into the private files of competitors is normal activity in the business community.

Most people, however, do not sit at these opposite poles. Many viewers will actively negotiate their interpretation out of a complex mix of experience and ideology. Business people may call upon their own experience to resist the premise that to be successful, a business person must be dishonest and heartless. Yet, their immediate experience may not extend to the market in general or to Wall Street traders. While they do not fit within Hollywood's image of the business personae, they may still accept the portrayal of the business world in general. Many viewers, however, will have no interpretive framework by which to actively resist such messages. Though virtually everyone in the industrialized context engages in the market process, markets are so ubiquitous that they usually escape our attention. In fact, we tend to only think about markets when our plans are frustrated, not the great majority of times when we are able to fulfill our plans through the market order. It is conceivable that a person who benefits from the market every day, perhaps even invests in a pension fund managed on Wall Street, may still accept the premise of a film like *Wall*

Street, that to be successful in business, one must be unethical and have boundless greed.

When it comes to the portrayal of African Americans, women, and homosexuals in film and on television, modern audiences have adopted developed structures of resistance that have allowed them to challenge and ultimately reshape popular culture. Yet, we would argue that a structure of resistance that would allow a similar critique of how business people are portrayed in popular culture does not yet widely exist. For instance, Gerbner (1984) found a positive and significant correlation between the acceptance of the negative image of business people and the average amount of television watched per day. As Gerbner's work suggests, without a framework by which such messages might be resisted, audiences are more likely to uncritically accept the implied message.

Further, Putnam (1996: 48) argues that television has been responsible for a significant decline in American social capital over the past thirty years. Not only has it displaced the time which might otherwise have been spent cultivating social networks, evidence suggests that it fosters greater skepticism and passivity towards community action. Given the negative portrayals of business on television and that the average American child watches about 40 hours of television per week it is not surprising that young people are particularly skeptical that one can be both moral and a successful business person. According to a study of New York City high school students, treachery and ruthlessness are believed to be necessary in order to achieve business success (London 1987).

This should not be surprising, given that the businessman antagonist is often not only portrayed as evil, but seductively so. The Gordon Gekko character in *Wall Street* is a case in point. If given the choice, many people would rather be the powerful Gordon Gekko, character flaws and all, than the reformed Bud Fox. Massing (1987: 97) found that among some *Dallas* viewers, JR "sparks their admiration for a macho ideal. They would like to dare being as unscrupulously cunning and aggressive and get away with it as he does. They are not like him, but they wish they were." We are not denying the potential for audiences to resist such cultural messages, but a structure and framework for such resistance does not seem to have emerged to any great extent.

5.2.3   Popular culture and the state

Even among cultural studies scholars who recognize the significant role popular culture plays in the evolution of social norms and belief systems, many might question whether the negative portrayal of business is really something to worry about. Some might argue that this is one case in which the repressed truth – that business people really are a bunch of crooks – seems to be bubbling up. Though the preferred meaning that usually emerges is one that supports the dominant culture, here might be a rare case in which the exploitative behavior of business is dramatized in the crimes and conspiracies of business characters. Still, others might respond by asking "so what?". If business is unfairly portrayed in popular culture, what difference will it make? After all, casting business characters as thieves and murderers is a lot like calling White people "honky" or "cracker". Yes, it is an insult, but the insult does not stick. The power and privilege enjoyed by the business elite is so pervasive, that no matter how unflattering the business characters appear, the messages received through popular culture will not undermine their position of privilege.

Yet, these interpretations miss two important points. First, they reveal a curious perception of just how much power the average business person really has. Perhaps because cultural studies evolved out of the traditional left, it still harbors the Marxist notion that business people run the system. In a moment we will consider the dangerous alliance between protected industry and the state, but first consider the average business person. As Lichter *et al.* (1997) point out, it is the operators of small businesses who received much of the worst treatment at the hands of Hollywood producers and scriptwriters. Yet, how much power do, say, West African entrepreneurs engaged in indigenous market trading really have? How much power does a bakery owner, or the owner of a hardware store have? Their only chance of earning a profit is to meet the needs of customers, either with lower prices, or with superior service and quality. If they consistently fail to do this, they are out of business. Running a small or medium-sized business hardly appears to be the same thing as "running the system."

Even chains like WalMart and Home Depot, much maligned for the competition they pose to smaller downtown shops, are extremely limited in their power. In fact, their power goes no further than the agency exercised by consumers. We are not suggesting that WalMarts and other similar organizations do not sometimes cause significant upheaval in communities. Nor are we suggesting that such organizations share none of the responsibility for the consequences of their success. What we are suggesting is that it is the power exercised by consumers that ultimately determines the success or failure of these organizations.

Secondly, these Hollywood interpretations of business power ignore a more insidious dynamic at work within the intersection between business and politics. To the extent that some businesses use their political influence to by-pass the discipline imposed by market forces, popular images of business may play a significant role in maintaining that position of privilege and power. Popular culture sets business and profit making up as a malevolent force within society that needs to be controlled and curtailed. Simultaneously, popular culture sets government up as the obvious institution that will counteract and mitigate the deleterious effects of business. Yet, rather than dismantling the power and privilege within the market, government intervention tends more often to create and maintain positions of privilege, as it eliminates the competition that would otherwise act as a discipline on private market behavior.

In popular culture texts, this dynamic is missed almost entirely. Rather, government is cast as an essentially benevolent force, and one that is exceptionally efficient when the "right people" are in charge. In the 1993 film *Dave*, protagonist Dave Kovic runs a small temporary agency in Washington, D.C. He would be just another average guy if it were not for the fact that he bears a striking resemblance to the United States President Bill Mitchell. Circumstances conspire and Dave finds himself fooling the entire country as he serves in Mitchell's place. Wary at first, he quickly realizes that he can do tremendous good with all this power. He provides houses for the homeless and jobs for all Americans who want them. He even manages to cut $650 million from the federal budget by proper money management and cutting boondoggle funding such as consumer confidence campaigns for the American auto industry. While the establishment in Washington is corrupt, in Hollywood government is capable of providing solutions, such as eliminating homelessness and unemployment, by the stroke of a pen.

The impression Hollywood has of government is at one time both gravely cynical and idealistically optimistic. On the one hand, the personae of the corrupt politician is an important source of material for Hollywood screenwriters. Though not nearly as frequently as business people, politicians are depicted as corrupt and despicable vermin. Eddie Murphy's character in the movie *The Distinguished Gentleman* quickly learns that players in Washington, D.C. are not committed to principles and causes. They are committed to the sources of political contributions. The centers of political power are devoid of any and all integrity.

Given this bleak portrayal of American governance, one might expect that positive political characters in film and television would be just as rare as positive business characters. Yet, in fact, they are not so rare. Out of the morally bankrupt world of American government emerge political characters who exemplify the highest ideals of a democratic and enlightened society. These characters push against the tide of special interests and pressures from the political establishment. In one sense, there is nothing so remarkable here. The idealist battling a corrupt system is a tried and true story line. What is noteworthy, however, is that once the positive political characters are in charge, the government works efficiently and only to the betterment of the society. Kevin Kline's character in the movie *Dave* seems to defy the very existence of scarcity through positive government action. It is only corrupt attitudes within government that drive inefficiency and bad policy.

Since, in Hollywood's perception, much of what is wrong in society is the ills perpetuated by the business community, government is then cast as protector of society against the interests of business. In its representation of business, Hollywood is not only depicting individual business people as morally flawed, it is implying that the pursuit of profit itself is loathsome and base. This is not the same for government. Political players are often portrayed as corrupt and unprincipled, but the system itself is rarely, if ever, challenged. Many movies about politics – whether *Mr. Smith Goes to*

Washington, *Harry's War*, or *Protocol* – feature corrupt politicians and civil servants, but then the situation is resolved by higher-ranking politicians with the proper moral agenda.

In the rare cases in which government itself is portrayed as sinister, the government is still portrayed as remarkably efficient. In the *X-Files* film and television series, the government conducts secret experiments that cause cancer and other diseases, reminiscent of the Tuskeege and uranium experiments conducted from the 1930s to the 1970s. Yet, just as a powerful state can do great evil, in the *X-Files*, a powerful state also has the capacity to cure everything from inoperable brain tumors to lung cancer, if only they used their power for good rather than evil. Similarly, in the film *Wag the Dog*, the government stages a war with Albania in order to save the President's approval rating in the face of a sex scandal. Like a puppet master, the powers of government flawlessly manipulate the American public, apparently with no negative unintended consequences. Though this is a more cynical perspective of government, it still supports the notion that if the right people were in charge, the government would be capable of solving any problem, including the evils perpetuated by business.

To the extent that the negative portrayal of business within popular culture supports a greater regulatory role for government in the economy, it also helps to maintain the privileged position enjoyed by businesses which are protected by political forces. Ironically, it is not within the unfettered market environment that business enterprises achieve a position of illegitimate power. In a competitive market environment, the power of business is limited by the agency exerted by consumers, suppliers, and labor. On the other hand, the more government involves itself in the economy, the greater the opportunity existing businesses have to secure special privilege and protection within the political apparatus. Existing businesses with political access will, for example, help craft regulatory legislation in such a way that it protects them from would-be competition. It is political protections and subsidies, not the unfettered forces of the market, that convey positions of power and privilege to the business elite. Ironically, by perpetuating the perception that government regulation attenuates the power and privilege of business, popular culture feeds into the perpetuation of the existing power structure.

5.3   A new cultural reading of business

As criticisms of how African Americans were portrayed in film and television first emerged, undoubtedly, many argued that no one would ever accept a serious Black character; that Blacks could only play the role of the buffoon. Series such as *The Cosby Show*, *I'll Fly Away*, *South Central* and many others have certainly changed some minds on this issue. The question is whether the same is possible for the portrayal of business people. The main stumbling block may first appear to be that an honest business character could never be a fruitful source of action, humor, or intrigue. Yet, if novelists and doctors can solve murders, why not business people? If oil refinery workers and housewives can make us laugh without demeaning either pursuit, why not business owners?

Though still exceedingly rare, we can point to several recent films that tell the stories of business people and have also enjoyed commercial and/or critical success. In the 1997 film *Jerry Macguire*, Tom Cruise plays the role of a sports agent forced to start all over again. The film draws us into the drama, not only of the budding romance between Jerry and his assistant, but also of the risks, set-backs, and triumphs of being an entrepreneur.

By appealing to the film industry to present business and business people more positively, we are not suggesting that business heroes need to be as attractive as Tom Cruise or have flawless characters. In the 1992 film *Other People's Money*, Danny DeVito plays Lawrence Garfield, a lecherous doughnut-eating Wall Street shark, who claims to love money more than anything or anyone. Even with all his faults, Larry presents a powerful case for why the search for profits is a noble pursuit. His adversary, Andrew Jorgenson, or "Jorgy" presents us with another positive image of business. Jorgy is the beloved founder of New England Wire and Cable, the company Larry is attempting to take over. Though Jorgy is portrayed as more naïve than most business people are, he makes the case that when done right, a place of business is part of what makes up community, and that to a lot of people, even to many stock holders, business is more than just dividends.

Similarly, in the 1998 film *You've Got Mail*, business is portrayed not as a world in which pure good meets pure evil, but as an arena in which all of our values are contested. The story centers around a discount book chain owned by Joe Fox moving in around the corner from a small children's bookstore that is owned by Catherine Kelley. Though the discount chain store is often portrayed in unflattering terms throughout the film, both characters present positive images of what it means to be in business. While Catherine's commitment to exceptional quality and service contributes to the character of the neighborhood, there is also something noble in making reading more affordable and accessible. Most surprisingly of all is that writer and director Nora Ephron does not end the film by finding some way to keep Catherine's bookstore in business or have Joe close his bookstore down. She manages to still portray Joe Fox sympathetically, even though he does what business people do: search for profits.

Yet, these stories are the exception. The notion that honest business people are just not interesting enough to feature in our stories is a by-product of the much larger issue. If popular images of business people are to be transformed, a paradigmatic shift is required in the way all players in the creation of meaning read the world of business.

Fortunately, we have examples for how such paradigmatic shifts can take place within popular culture. Though the ABC network has canceled the program, the series *Ellen* is still a model for how archetypal representations can be transformed within popular culture. For decades, the only gay and lesbian characters appearing on television were more clichés than characters. Perhaps because of a growing distaste for such clichés, or simply because there is only so much mileage screenwriters can derive from lampooning gay stereotypes, positive lesbian and gay characters eventually made their way onto prime-time series such as *Friends* and *Spin City*. The commercial success of the show *Ellen* and the growing sensitivity to lesbian and gay concerns in general, gave actress and writer Ellen Degeneres the leverage she needed to have her character come out, as she herself had done in real life.

Even the relatively short-lived success of such shows suggests that mainstream audiences have developed greater awareness regarding gay and lesbian issues, at least to the extent that they can more actively resist the messages embedded within gay and lesbian stereotypes. Along the way, the screenwriters for shows featuring positive lesbian and gay characters have taken advantage of the emerging sense that to be a sophisticated person, one should be able to detect homophobic behavior and attitudes. The show *Ellen* pokes fun not only at characters who expect lesbians to be interested in automobile maintenance, but also at characters who display their "progressive style" by letting the world know that they have a gay friend. In this way, the screenwriters manage to educate heterosexual audiences that it is not appropriate to flaunt one's gay friends as if they were the latest fashion, yet at the same time, they let the audience play insider to the joke, allowing the viewer to say "I can laugh because I would never do such a thing." Though the show suffered backlash within the popular press and within its own network, the interplay between audience, text, and screenwriter has nonetheless exerted a powerful force within the dominant culture.

If business characters in film and television are to make the same sort of progress that lesbian and gay characters are beginning to make, a similar sort of transformation has to occur in the minds of those who construct the meaning of popular culture texts. Producers and screenwriters certainly have a role to play in this, simply by choosing to create positive business characters. Before Ellen Morgan was breaking ground for lesbian characters on television, she was breaking ground for business characters. In the second season of *Ellen*, the writers saw the opportunity for plot and character development by having Ellen buy the bookstore in which she worked from her self-centered boss. Ellen represented one of the few positive portrayals of a business owner on prime-time television.

Yet initiatives made by screenwriters and producers will not be enough. If the meaning embedded within popular culture texts is to be challenged, audiences will also have to cultivate a more critical framework by which to read such texts. In the last season of the program, *Ellen*, the lead character sold her bookstore to a faceless national chain in order to purchase a modest but comfortable home. After selling the bookstore, she was demoted to assistant manager and a stuffy corporate type took control of the business she had built. From a business perspective, this text is so implausible that it borders on the ridiculous. First, it is highly unlikely that a young business owner would sell her only productive asset in order to purchase a home. Simply put, she would not have to. This is what banks do – they lend money to people who have the potential to pay it back. In fact, it seems more plausible that she would have been a better credit risk as a business owner than as an assistant manager. Secondly, if a corporation hires a former owner back as an employee, it is most likely for their local knowledge and expertise. It is highly unlikely that they would hire her back only to treat her so shabbily. To the extent that such texts go unchallenged, the audience is complicit in the perpetuation of implausible and negative portrayals of business.

Both economists and cultural studies scholars might – for different reasons – question our direct appeal to audiences to re-evaluate their interpretations of business characters in popular culture. Coming from the position that economics ought to be a value-free science, many economists might argue that persuading audiences to have a different read of popular culture oversteps the bounds of the social scientist. But we would respond by arguing that a value-free social science is impossible, since the interpretive process that is social science requires that we engage on the level of values, both our own as investigators, as well as those held by the participants in the market process. Further, professional and academic economists are always in the business of persuasion. We try to persuade policy makers and voters that this or that economic policy is the one that makes the most sense. Using mathematical models, graphs, and just plain talk, we try to persuade students to see the market as a process of coordination, i.e., to see things from the economist's perspective. The economist's claim of value-freedom is an empty one.

The notion of a value-free social science would find few allies within cultural studies, as here it is recognized that the particular position the investigator holds within the social structure is a critical part of what informs the investigation. Yet critics from cultural studies might argue that in making a direct appeal to the audience to cultivate greater awareness of how business people and the business world are portrayed in popular culture, we are in danger of superimposing a rarefied and disconnected academic reading onto ordinary and everyday interpretation. Hayward (1997), Jenkins (1992), and others working within fan culture take issue with academic feminists, for example, who in effect criticize audience interpretation as not being radical enough, thus creating a need for academic feminists to intervene on their behalf. The important move being made here is that Hayward and others are calling attention to the ways in which an ideology meant to dismantle patriarchal power structures often reasserts patriarchy in the form of academic elitism.

> ... [S]oap operas have been derided as a mindless and archetypal "female" narrative form; and disturbingly, even feminist studies of soap operas and other "women's genres" have contributed to this disdain. Tania Modleski's *Loving with a Vengeance: Mass Produced Fantasies for Women*

provides perhaps the clearest example of the extent to which our desire, as academic feminists, to move beyond isolating theorization to achieve real social change can produce a paradoxical inability to respect the "objects" of our efforts, in this case, female consumers of mass culture. After acknowledging that soap operas address real social needs (for community among other things), Modleski closes her third chapter, "The Search for Tomorrow in Today's Soap Operas," with a call for action: "As feminists, we have a responsibility to devise ways of meeting these needs that are more creative, honest, and interesting than the ones mass culture has supplied. Otherwise, the search for tomorrow threatens to go on, endlessly". (Hayward 1997: 9)

Similarly, Jenkins (1992: 6) criticizes traditional ethnographic methodology which calls for a distancing between the investigator and the subject.

In the past, scholars with little direct knowledge or emotional investment within the fan community have transformed fandom into a projection of their personal fears, anxieties, and fantasies about the dangers of mass culture. This more distanced perspective did not ensure a better understanding of the complexity of the phenomenon so much as it enabled scholars to talk about a group presumed incapable of responding to their representation. This same danger recurs in more recent and substantially more sympathetic treatment of fan culture, such as Janice Radway's otherwise exemplary *Reading the Romance* (1984), which cast [academic feminist] writers as vanguard intellectuals who might lead the fans toward a more overtly political relationship to popular culture. Academic distance has thus allowed scholars either to judge or to instruct but not to converse with the fan community, a process which requires greater proximity and the surrender of certain intellectual pretensions and institutional privileges.

In appealing directly to audiences to adopt a more critical and reflective interpretive framework by which to assess the portrayal of business in popular culture, we may be in danger of perpetuating the same academic elitism that Hayward and Jenkins are addressing. If all we do as academic critics of popular culture is tell audiences what to think, we have replicated the very paternalism cultural studies seeks to undermine. But Hayward's and Jenkins' cautions should not be read as appeals for self-censorship. Silencing any direct appeal from academics (such as ourselves) to audiences would be just as problematic as the elitism we hope to avoid. Any call to cut off the dialogue implies that the agency enjoyed by viewers in determining the meaning of popular culture texts is so vulnerable and so tenuous, that it could not stand up to a challenge coming from the academic arena.

The next question, then, is how audiences might go about cultivating a framework by which implausible and negative images of business characters are challenged? The most potent source for cultivating critical readings of business in popular culture is everyday lived experience. We engage in market activity virtually every day. The enormous complexity of even the most common plans, everything from making a meal to reading a book, relies upon layers and layers of market coordination we never see. Being more reflective about all the ways in which markets enhance our daily living is an important place to start. Secondly, hearing stories can help cultivate tools for rethinking the messages received in popular culture. Talking with business people, hearing their stories of struggle, success, failure, and the everyday ins and outs of good business practice can also enrich our understanding of the norms which really operate in business communities.

Part of the answer can also be found in the ways that economists and business professionals tell their stories. Most economic theory virtually eliminates the human being from the stories it tells about the market. In the stories of mainstream economics, economic decisions are more like math problems than judgments. Decision-makers are more like automatons than human beings. If this is the image that the economics profession gives to business people, perhaps we should not be surprised by the negative portrayal of business in popular culture. At least on TV the business people are interesting, albeit despicable. In economic theory, we cannot even say that they are interesting. Fortunately, business schools have made much more progress in this area than the economics profession. The case study method favored by the leading business programs is beginning to tell more powerful human stories about the world of business. In the next chapter, we will tell some of the stories that may help cultivate a structure by which we might better resist the implied messages within popular culture. We will also explore the role cultural studies might play in understanding market activity as a central and meaningful part of human existence.

6 The market order and the moral order

In early religions, even those which otherwise placed a high positive value on the possession of wealth, purely commercial enterprises were practically always the objects of adverse judgment. . . .

. . .[I]t is above all the impersonal and economically rationalized (and for this very reason ethically irrational) character of purely commercial relationships that evokes the suspicion, never clearly expressed but all the more strongly felt, of ethical religions.

Max Weber ([1924] 1968: 584–5)

There is hardly an ethical problem, in fact, without its economic aspect. Our daily ethical decisions are in the main economic decisions, and nearly all our daily economic decisions have, in turn, an ethical aspect.

Henry Hazlitt (1964: 301)

Some economists would have us view business decision-making as simply a matter of mechanically responding to external forces, in such a way that issues of moral responsibility in business are ruled out of order. The entrepreneur does the bidding of the consumer, or is eliminated by market competition, period. This chapter presents a critique of mainstream economics, revisiting the debate as to what role ethical considerations can or should play in business. We will argue that this characterization of the market process presents the market as a closed text in which only the most narrowly defined choices can lead to economic success, thereby rendering opposing and radical reinterpretations impossible. The field of cultural studies ought to be particularly well-placed to see the market as instead a polysemic dialogue, a text that is open to a wide array of potential readings. It should be able to help us to challenge the notion that the only thing that matters in making business decisions is the "bottom line."

6.1 Unintended consequences and the ethics of business

In the study of markets and business, where does morality come in? From the very origins of political economy in the work of classical liberal moral philosophers, the moral defense of the market rested not on the individual's ability to intentionally improve the lives of others and the community in general, but rather on the idea of unintended consequences – that such benefits are conveyed despite the individual's interest in promoting his or her own interests. Yet the question of whether the unintended benefits of market activity relieve business from further obligations to serve society is far from resolved.

6.1.1   *The invisible hand and the minimalist argument*

The economist's contribution to this debate begins with Adam Smith's invisible hand thesis in which the self-interested choices of individuals in the market generate socially beneficial results, though these social benefits are not intended. The emphasis on unintended beneficial consequences has been such a strong theme of economics since Smith that contemporary economists seem to use it as a shield to deflect moral argument. Individuals need not be morally virtuous, they need only obey the law and pursue their own self-interest and good things will happen. This is what we shall call the *minimalist* defense of the morality of market decisions: that the only moral criterion to which business people can be held is that they operate within the limits of the law. To expect anything beyond this, it is argued, would undermine market efficiency and a free society.

This, by the way, was not the view of Adam Smith (see for example, [1759] 1984). While under certain conditions of the rule of law it can be argued that most of the results of business and entrepreneurship can be socially beneficial, Smith recognized that they are not all so. For example, Smith pointed to the deleterious effects of business seeking protection to insulate itself from competitive forces.

Further, some of a business's decisions might impose negative externalities on the community in which it operates, perhaps leading to a lower quality of life. Some management styles place tremendous pressures on employees and their families, which may contribute to escalating divorce rates. Business people do not necessarily intend for these things to happen, and the workers who experience such stress must bear some moral responsibility for remaining in a job that is destroying them, but surely the managers must bear some moral responsibility as well. If we are to credit business with the unintended benefits it conveys upon society, perhaps we should hold it accountable for the negative unintended consequences as well.

If economists are to argue that the market economy is moral, it may not be enough to say that business unintentionally serves the needs of society in general. Such a laudable result does not preclude society from also expecting intended socially beneficial action. The traditional moral defense of the market on unintended consequences grounds alone does not effectively argue against demands for businesses to act with a social conscience, while they also pursue profits.

We agree with the emphasis in the minimalist argument on the importance of property and contract law, and agree with many of the economists' answers to the business ethics community on the role of law. For market processes to generate economic prosperity, the law needs to be shaped to define domains of legitimate action, through the drawing of property rights boundaries, and through the development of contract law, all of which helps potential market participants to understand their permitted domain of action. The vague appeals for more moral behavior that pervade the business ethics literature often completely miss the significance of the simple ethics of obedience to well-defined legal commitments. When most participants to a market respect one another's property rights and honor contracts, enormous benefits can flow from this simply legal behavior.

But as important as obedience to the law is in the workings of markets, this need not be all one can say about business ethics. The mainstream economics framework tends to depict action as a matter of calculative choice, of the mechanical selection of the optimal alternative, leaving no "slack in the machinery" where one might find room for the exercise of moral judgment. Outside of these assumptions, however, the business person in the real world is often placed in situations that demand a fuller moral perspective.

6.1.2   Socialism, social responsibility, and the traditional defense of market morality

When Henry Hazlitt wrote *The Foundations of Morality* in the early 1960s, he saw as his main ideological opponents Marxists and other traditional socialists who characterized capitalism and markets as inherently evil. Traditional socialism advocated the abolition of market relations and their replacement by centralized economic planning. One could argue against this traditional socialist position, as did John Bates Clark in *The Distribution of Wealth* (1899) that the market economy is just, since on the margin, factors of production, including labor, tend to earn the value of what they create. But this defense ultimately relies on an efficiency argument. If one is to construct a persuasive argument against the socialist critique of alienation and exploitation, the task will involve more than a defense made on efficiency grounds. Hazlitt understood the persuasiveness of leftist ideology which portrayed markets as stripping away every layer of humanity from both worker and capitalist. To argue only that markets generate greater efficiency and wealth accumulation would be to miss the central charge that markets are fundamentally immoral.

Hazlitt argues that the market is premised upon a system of morality. Free enterprise necessitates mutual respect for private property and the corresponding freedom to employ property in the manner the owner deems most useful. Competition, when conducted within a context of a moral society, benefits both the individual competitors and society in general. Through competitive bidding, competitors "help" one another to become more efficient. Of course, this mutual assistance is not the intent, yet the results of lower costs, better information, and greater prosperity for society are nonetheless undeniable (Hazlitt 1964: 303–5). Hazlitt echoes Adam Smith's central point that it is not the intent that matters so much as the result. Widespread relief from poverty and famine more often comes through individuals following their self-interest as opposed to the general interest. It is this very action which seeks to satisfy self-interest that ultimately serves the greater society. Thus, there is no necessary contradiction between self-interest and altruism.

Similarly, F.A. Hayek argues in *The Fatal Conceit* that the social institutions of the market such as property, contract and law serve the general interest to a greater extent than any direct altruistic behavior ever could (Hayek 1988: 19). The market order is one best characterized as a cooperative process. Rivalry among business and entrepreneurs enables individuals to find mutually agreeable terms for resolving conflict, acquiring resources, and coordinating otherwise divergent plans. Centralized planning is incapable of replacing the knowledge-generating function served by private ownership and competitive markets, and where consistently pursued leads to a severe reduction in economic well-being.

These arguments lay the foundation for a persuasive case in favor of the morality of the market, particularly as opposed to traditional centralized-planning-based socialism. If we were to substitute "the best interest of society" for "the best interests of the individual" as the criterion for all production and distribution decisions, abject poverty would soon result. The fact that it would be a more egalitarian system is little comfort if everyone is equally miserable. By allowing individuals to follow their self-interest, the benefits that accrue to society make for a far more moral system than one that has altruistic intentions but devastating results. Thus, the traditional socialist is in a difficult position when it comes to arguing against the morality of the market economy, when one considers the practical results of each system.

Yet, most who currently argue that business has some kind of social responsibility beyond that of running a profitable business are not demanding the overthrow of the capitalist system. Among advocates of socially conscious business, wide consensus exists that without a profitable enterprise, business is incapable of engaging in any activity, philanthropic or otherwise. Further, most recognize that the functions of business benefit society as they generate profits for the individual. Unlike traditional socialists, advocates of the "socially responsible" business do not see wealth accumulation as the outcome of a necessarily exploitative process. The recent calls for business to be socially responsible, for example in the criticisms of Time Warner for selling "cop killer" rap, do not suggest that business and market relations are inherently immoral. Rather, such challenges speak to a belief that business is capable of advancing the moral order.

While Hazlitt's moral defense of the market is an argument against traditional socialism, it does not address the challenge that calls for greater social responsibility on the part of business. Clearly, the general interest cannot be the sole criterion for business decisions, but there is nothing in the moral defense of the market to suggest that business has no social responsibility. Sethi and Steidlmeier (1991), Makower (1994), Solomon (1994) and its argue that business does indeed have such responsibilities alongside its responsibility to obey the law and to try to run a profitable business.

6.1.3   *A renewed challenge to business*

The debate over what responsibility business owes society has been with us for a long time. The wealth and growth generated by the industrial revolution also generated debate as to the proper treatment of employees, honesty in dealings with consumers, and the proper stewardship of profits once earned. With the dawn of the industrial revolution, religious groups such as the Quakers saw a clear role for the successful businessman to play in the betterment of society. Quaker religious teachings reinforced the larger role an employer played in the nurturing and education of employees, for example. Members of the faith were sometimes "disowned" by the society if they were found to be conducting business in an unethical manner. Further, successful business owners were expected to enrich all of society through philanthropic endeavors.

Since the eighteenth century, the calls for business to be socially responsible have often fallen upon deaf ears. But the 1990s seem to have ushered in new calls for business persons to make decisions with a social conscience. According to Sethi and Steidlmeier (1991: xiv), co-authors of *Up Against the Corporate Wall*, a widely used text in management degree programs, corporations must take the lead in socially progressive causes.

> The corporation must become an active agent for social change. The corporation cannot confine its role to responding to societal goals advocated by other groups. As a dominant institution in society, it must assume its rightful place and contribute to the articulation of the public agenda itself. In today's pluralistic society, corporate participation in social policy formulation is not a luxury but a necessity; it must receive top management attention and the corporate resources to do it right and to do it well.

Robert Solomon (1994: 4–5), author of *The New World of Business: Ethics and Free Enterprise in the Global 1990s* observes that the tide has indeed already changed in favor of the socially responsible business. Solomon argues that ethicists have as much, if not more, to say about business decision-making than economists.

> The turn into the 1990s has thus brought with it a healthy and refreshing self-examination, reflection on the principles and preconditions of a truly

free market, debate about the presuppositions and meaning of prosperity and the obligations that go along with it. . . Ethics has replaced economics as the first language of business, and the current self examination, reflection and debate are healthy alternatives to the narrow-minded focus on "the market." It is people that count, first of all. Profits and products, corporations and markets, are secondary and subservient.

Joel Makower (1994: 18), author of *Beyond the Bottom Line* observes that the climate in which business is to be conducted as we make our way into the 21st century has fundamentally changed. Business is not just beholden to customers and stockholders. Business is now seen to have a much wider constituency to which it is responsible.

No longer is it sufficient for [business owners] to obey the law and pay [their] taxes. Tomorrow's successful companies increasingly will be asked to take a hard look at the impact of their operations both within and beyond their institutional walls, more carefully scrutinize the impact of a variety of policies on employees, customers, communities, and society as a whole.

Nothing less than a fundamental change is being promoted within these and other treatises on social responsibility and the role of business. Some market advocates charge that requiring business to meet social needs is tantamount to socialism, and will eventually result in the collapse of both the market order and the moral order. Others argue that the continued vitality of markets will depend upon individual firms taking on greater social responsibility. We will argue that neither side of this argument has adequately answered what role business ought to play in social life.

6.2   The minimalist defense of the market

A line of defense most economists have used to try to insulate business from calls for greater social responsibility has been to argue that, apart from the matter of obedience to the law, business is neither moral nor immoral, but amoral. The legal rules within which markets work can be accused of being immoral, such as in a market for slavery, but markets as such are neutral tools that moral and immoral persons deploy. Since moral responsibility can only be attached to persons, a business enterprise as such cannot be moral or immoral. And as for the manager within a business, she needs to be thought of as merely an agent in a principal/agent relationship, representing the interests of her employers, ultimately the stockholders. Her moral choice is only that of choosing whether to adhere to the terms of the contract or quit, but insofar as she acts in her capacity as an agent of the stockholders, her behavior is amoral. How about the stockholders? They can in turn be viewed as agents of their bosses, the consumers. This point of view leaves little room for morality in business life.

6.2.1   *The morality of obedience to stockholders*

In his *Common Sense of Political Economy*, Philip Wicksteed (1910: 184–5) offered an early defense of this position.

> It is idle to assume that ethically desirable results will necessarily be produced by an ethically indifferent instrument, and it is foolish to make the economic relation an idol as it is to make it a bogey. The world has many things that I want for myself and others, and that I can get only by some kind of exchange. What, then, have I, or what can I do or make, that the world wants? Or what can I make it want, or persuade it that it wants, or make it believe that I can give it better than others can? The things I want, if measured by an ideal standard, may be good or bad for me to have or for others to give; and so with the things I give them, the desires I stimulate in them, and the means I employ to gratify them. When we draw the seductive picture of "economic harmony" in which everyone is "helping" someone else and making himself "useful" to him, we insensibly allow the idea of "help" to smuggle in with it ethical or sentimental associations that are strictly contraband.

According to this argument, the market has no moral content, whatsoever. The market is an instrument by which individuals match means to their various ends. Those ends may be laudable and morally upright or they may be base and sinister. The instrument by which means are put to these ends lies beyond moral scrutiny.

Milton Friedman employed this theme to exempt business from having any social responsibility save that of pursuing profits within the framework of rights established in law. In *Capitalism and Freedom* and *The New York Times Magazine* essay, "The Social Responsibility of Business," Friedman (1962, 1970), argues that only individuals, not businesses, can be said to have responsibilities. A corporate manager may have personal responsibilities. But as an agent of the corporation, he has no responsibilities other than to maximize the returns to the owners of the company. To argue otherwise is to argue that the corporate manager should do something other than conduct the company's affairs in the best interest of his employers. According to Friedman (1970 [1987]: 38) if the manager were to serve environmentalist ends, hire an employee other than the best qualified person willing to accept the position, or give profits to charitable causes, this would be tantamount to theft, as he is essentially being generous with somebody else's money.

> In each of these cases, the corporate executive would be spending someone else's money for a general social interest. Insofar as his actions in accord with his "social responsibility" reduce returns to stockholders, he is spending their money. Insofar as his actions raise the price to

customers, he is spending the customers' money. Insofar as his actions lower the wages of some employees, he is spending their money. . . [H]e is in effect imposing taxes on the one hand, and deciding how the tax proceeds shall be spent, on the other.

In keeping with his passionate defense of liberty, Friedman argues that stockholders, employees, and customers should not be forced to pay for the social causes advocated by others. Again, Friedman is not arguing that managers should not pursue social causes as private citizens, but simply that as an agent of the corporation, there is only one duty – profit maximization (subject to the constraints imposed by the rights of others).

Friedman recognizes that some businesses may benefit by cloaking themselves in the blanket of social responsibility. If profits are to be found by this strategy, he does not begrudge firms from pursuing the opportunity. Yet Friedman does worry about the unintended consequences of such actions. To deploy the rhetoric of the socially conscious business is to perpetuate the view that the pursuit of profits is fundamentally base and evil. As this perception is reinforced, Friedman predicts that the cries to mitigate and control the damage business inflicts upon society in its pursuit of profits will proliferate. As government regulation grows, business decisions will be increasingly made according to bureaucratic, not business principles. To add insult to injury, this increased bureaucratic control has little chance of actually advancing social ends. The negative unintended consequences of government intervention, such as wage and price controls, ultimately harm the very people the policies are proposed to help.

The minimalist defense that Wicksteed and Friedman offer does not mean that they are unconcerned about morality. First of all they strongly endorse the morality of legality, of respect for the legally defined rights of others. Secondly they point to morally good results that unintentionally arise from market processes. To suggest that individual business decisions be made upon the grounds of market efficiency and maximizing the returns to stockholders is consistent with the notion that unintended social benefits emerge from private self-interested choices. Further, it is the value of freedom that they seek to preserve. Ultimately, they argue, to hold business responsible for social problems is to argue against the foundations of a free society. When the decision to commit financial support to a particular cause or social movement is taken away from the individual, we have not arrived at a more socially just society. We have simply forfeited our liberty. We will suggest, however, that things are not that simple.

6.2.2   *From stockholders to stakeholders*

The minimalist defense of the market is an attempt to insulate the market from the demands that business executives consider criteria beyond those that will enhance profitability (and obey the laws). Yet recent literature on the subject questions whether it is even possible to be in business and divorce oneself from morality and ethics. As Solomon (1994: 11) suggests:

> . . . ethics isn't a set of absolute principles divorced from and imposed on everyday life. Ethics is a way of life, a seemingly delicate but in fact very strong tissue of endless adjustments and compromises. It is the awareness that one is an intrinsic part of a social order, in which the interests of others and one's own interests are inevitably intertwined. And what is business, you should ask, if not precisely that awareness of what other people want and need, and how you yourself can prosper by providing it?. . . Business isn't a single-minded pursuit of profits; it is an *ethos*, a way of life. It is a way of life that is at its very foundation ethical.

To build a case in favor of an economy inhabited by socially conscious businesses, business ethicists have developed the concept of the "stakeholder" (see Sturdivant and Vernon-Wrotzel 1990). At the start, such analysis assumes that the firm is a social and political reality, and as such serves a multitude of constituencies. Stockholders, employees, customers, suppliers, distributors, the local, national and global communities are all potential stakeholders in the firm (Danley 1994: 163–4). While stockholders are important players in a company's decision, there is no necessary reason, according to stakeholder analysis, that the stockholder's interests must always prevail over the interests of employees, customers, the environment or the community. Stakeholder analysis assumes that these various constituencies should all be weighed and balanced against each other along with considerations for corporate profitability. Implicit in stakeholder analysis is the argument that a socially responsible firm will sometimes make decisions that favor one or more of these constituencies over profits, that is, over the interests of shareholders (Danley 1994: 191).

Fundamental to the case in favor of social responsibility is the fact that firms have impacts on a variety of constituencies. This impact is certainly often positive in that the firm satisfies a demand in the marketplace, generates gainful employment, and in general contributes to society. Yet, the impact can be negative, and might lead to the disruption of social life. As Solomon puts it:

> . . .[E]very corporation has impact and so faces questions concerning compliance, contribution, and consequences. Those questions are the essence of social responsibility. There is no such thing as impact without social responsibility, and a company that is without impact is a company that is already out of business. (Solomon 1994: 213)

Solomon adds that the extent to which the firm is responsible will always be a matter of debate since the degree of culpability and the availability of alternative courses of action will depend upon the particular circumstances. But the fact that business executives have some responsibility is not in question.

Practical reasons might also be considered for business to act with a social conscience. In particular, it often pays for a firm to pursue a socially progressive agenda. Though the evidence is mixed, demonstrated concern for the community, employees, customers and the environment is often rewarded with increased sales, a more loyal work force, or a better public relations image (Solomon 1994: 209). A 1994 study conducted at Florida International University found a positive and significant relationship between social responsibility and growth in sales and returns on assets. Another 1994 study conducted by the Gordon Group of Waban, Massachusetts found a positive and significant correlation between a high reputation for equitable and humane workplace practices and higher price-to-book valuation ratios, relative to similar firms in the industry. Firms which ranked lowest in terms of workplace practices were more likely to experience bankruptcy (Makower 1994: 73). The inevitable correlation versus causation question arises here. Does a socially responsible agenda generate profits, or are successful companies simply more likely to engage in socially progressive programs because they can "afford" to? Indeed, both causal directions may be operative. The more important point is that these studies suggest that a socially responsible agenda does not have to place the firm in jeopardy, and perhaps may help the firm to succeed.

Though Solomon (1994), Makower (1994), and most other contributors to stakeholder analysis agree with Friedman that business cannot be expected to solve all the problems that confront society, they nonetheless argue that business has a pivotal role to play in social progress. They argue that Friedman's assertion that the sole task of the corporate manager is to maximize returns to shareholders is flawed. "Executives are also hired – and fired – for the reputation they give to and earn for a company. Executives are expected to make life agreeable for the hundreds of thousands of employees of the company – and not only to increase productivity and avoid lawsuits" (Solomon 1994: 214). To be fair to Friedman, he would agree that these may also be important considerations, but mainly in so far as they may indirectly effect long-run returns.

Although ultimately it can be argued that only individuals, not collective entities such as "business," can be held responsible, part of the reason the corporation was invented was to create a responsible legal entity. The minimalist position agrees with the stakeholder view that (individuals who make decisions on behalf of) corporations need to respect the legal responsibilities involved, so that in some sense one can say that the corporation must take responsibility to obey the law. Solomon (1994: 215) argues further.

> But if corporations have social responsibilities in this kind of case, it must make sense to say that they have responsibilities in other senses, too. If the corporation is a citizen of society, why should it not have the responsibility to enrich (as well as to avoid harming) that society? Of

course, it has often been argued that individuals do not have any obligation to enrich society either, as if it were enough not to cause harm and to leave other people alone. But when one is as powerful as even a minor corporation, it is hard to "leave other people alone," and in any case, we would be a pretty poor society if no one felt compelled except by way of whimsy to enrich society and not just take from it.

There is much to challenge in the stakeholders argument, but it appears that the minimalist defense of the market leaves itself open to serious critique. The argument that business is inextricably linked with questions of ethics and morality is the crucial point advanced by stakeholder analysis, and it is here that the analysis begins to question the foundations of the minimalist argument. The conclusion that morally informed business decisions will result in inefficiency falls directly out of mainstream economics and its equilibrium-oriented assumptions. We wish to develop this critique and present an alternative approach to understanding the role of morality in business decisions. But first, it is important to point out some of the shortcomings of the stakeholder argument.

First, we question the criterion of "impact" as a useful guidepost for the socially conscientious firm. It is not at all clear that the firm will necessarily know the impact it has on all the various constituencies. Who *exactly* are the stakeholders of any particular firm? Through social activism, legal disputes and media reports, businesses might know some of the groups which they affect, but certainly not all. This is not to suggest that in the absence of perfect information, the firm should do nothing. The point is that "impact" is not an objectively defined standard that will unambiguously dictate a course of action. Even if the firm were able unambiguously to identify its stakeholders and the impact it imposes upon them, what to do about it will rarely be a simple matter. In some cases it may be clear what projects a company might pursue, but this will certainly not always be the case. If a company operates in an area of increasing crime rates, how exactly is it supposed to help the local community, given that it has no control over the local police or court system? It may decide to establish a community youth program to stem teen violence. But will this project have more or less impact in curbing crime, relative to a program designed to retrain displaced workers? Much of the stakeholder literature sounds as if the proper course of action will be obvious. In this sense, it suffers from the same modernistic notion mainstream economics is crippled by: that the "right" decisions are objectively defined.

Like profit opportunities themselves, the ways in which business people might effect positive social change need to be interpreted out of a complex social, political, and cultural context in which no single course of action presents itself as the only correct choice. In many cases the judicious mix of business and social activism may have nothing to do with "impact." In 1992, Alan Rappaport, owner of Julius Klein Cleaners in New York City offered to clean one suit or dress per week for any unemployed worker free of charge until they found a new position (Scott and Rothman 1994: 200). If impact had been Rappaport's main criterion for social activism, he might have directed some of his profits to correct the environmental damage dry cleaning chemicals cause. Instead, he built upon the infrastructure that was already in place, so as to help those in his community more directly. Similarly, Trailways Bus Service instituted a program called "Home-Free," in which runaways could travel back to their parents free of charge (Solomon 1994: 206). Of course Trailways is not responsible for children running away, yet its infrastructure allows it to serve a social good at a relatively low cost. Further, distinct social and religious commitments act as the guiding criteria for many socially progressive businesses. The Greyston Bakery supplies gourmet pastries to some of New York's most renowned restaurants. The company also provides housing, job training, and counseling services for nearby low-income residents. The vision for Greyston's social activism was provided by its founder, a Zen Buddhist priest. Again, if impact were the principal criterion, perhaps Greyston ought to have provided nutritional counseling for wealthy restaurant patrons who eat too many pastries. The owner's religious convictions provided a much different interpretation of how he could use his business to effect positive social change.

As a criterion for correcting harm that a business might impose, "impact" poses other problems as well. It makes no distinction between harm that justifies corrective action and harm that does not. It seems relatively clear that if a product causes severe illness and the company fails to warn consumers of the potential danger, the company should be held liable for damages. On the other hand, if a product creates a mild annoyance to some, such as the too sweet smell of a cookie factory, most would agree that such an annoyance is not actionable. Yet, holding to the concept of "impact necessitates responsibility," we could not make such distinctions. Responsibility in this context extends far beyond the parameters set by the legal process. Thus, contrary to ethicists' sensible caveat that business is not responsible for all social problems, the field seems dangerously wide open for an infinite variety of claims in the name of "impact." Stakeholder analysis makes no systematic distinction between major liability claims and minor side effects and externalities. The disappointment a distributor experiences when a production line is cancelled would have to count as "impact" just as missed family meals would count when employees work late to please a client or a supervisor. By the logic of stakeholder analysis, such impact makes legitimate any claim society has on the company to engage in corrective or compensatory action.

Further, the notion of "impact" runs roughshod over the distinction between "doing harm," and "failing to benefit." As Friedman argues, this distinction is the cornerstone of a free society. Self sovereignty requires the ability to refuse action. A system of slavery is premised upon the notion that one can legitimately force another to engage in action he or she would not pursue voluntarily. A free society is premised on the opposite notion – that one cannot legitimately be forced to serve the purposes of others. The fact that those purposes might often be noble and worthwhile in some abstract sense makes no difference. To do away with the principle of voluntary action, no matter how worthy the end, is to annihilate freedom and to institute slavery. When the challenge of social responsibility is made in the arena of civic debate, this is no longer a problem, as any action taken in response to those claims would be voluntary. But when such claims of social responsibility are to be enforced through government edicts, Friedman's cautions become legitimate concerns.

The problems with stakeholder analysis do not mean that the argument in favor of socially responsible business is without merit, however. Values cannot simply be turned off once inside the corporate world. Mainstream economics creates a misleading image of what good management is, suggesting that managers are mere puppets of anonymous "market forces," rather than thoughtful decision-makers.

And it is not only mainstream economists who treat managerial decision-making as if ethics had nothing to do with it. Many are misled by an undeniable feature of global markets, the increase in impersonal exchange relations. The rise of capitalistic society involves a marked increase in more impersonal relationships, where the persons responsible for producing the goods and services we enjoy are less likely than ever before in history to be people we know personally. But this does not mean that all the personal relationships disappear, or that even the highly impersonal ones are outside of ethical considerations. When Max Weber, in the quotation at the opening of this chapter, refers to "the impersonal and economically rationalized (and for this very reason ethically irrational) character of purely commercial relationships" the parenthetical remark needs to be interrogated. Where impersonal commercial relationships arise because of their economic rationality, where we buy a Sony TV because it is cheap, even though we do not know the Japanese workers who made it, does this necessarily mean these relationships are ethically irrational, are beyond the pale of moral discourse? Is it not, in fact, precisely our ethical obligation to apply ethical reasoning to all the domains of our lives, to the way we conduct ourselves in the workplace and in the marketplace, with regard to strangers from foreign lands as well as to intimates?

Cultural studies scholars recognize the potential for decision-makers to resist preferred meanings within the dominant culture, even when they are responding out of that culture. Managers are hired to make difficult decisions, not to follow orders blindly. They are hired with the understanding that they will have some *discretion* in their decision-making, otherwise why hire them at all? Managerial discretion means that the values that come from the culture will be brought to bear upon business decisions, even those that will affect the bottom line. Certainly, most economists know that managers are hired to make difficult and complex decisions. But the equilibrium assumptions of mainstream thinking keep us from exploring this role of managerial discretion as anything other than a deviation from the singularly correct path of profit maximizing.

6.3   Markets and the construction of meaning

The argument that no scope exists for social responsibility in business (aside from the responsibility we all have to obey the law) falls directly out of the equilibrium assumptions of mainstream economics. Within the model of perfect competition, there is no room for interpretation, no space for weighing alternatives, no slack. Agents in such a world are mere cogs in the machine, never really exhibiting any true agency. As such, morality rarely enters into the stories told by mainstream economics. Socially embedded subjects in the real world, on the other hand, grope to read profits out of a complex environment, and to interpret meanings held by others in a world shrouded in uncertainty, and fragmented into diverse perspectives. By recasting the market as a sort of open text, we recognize that a variety of readings can be constructed out of the same data. As new readings of the market emerge, some may have the potential to challenge the dominant culture. We think that this is a move that will be of particular interest to cultural studies scholars because it opens up the everyday world of market interaction as a potential site of resistant readings that can lead to social change.

6.3.1   Room for moral choices

At the heart of mainstream economic analysis rests the explicit assumption that economic agents possess (or come to possess) all relevant information necessary to make rational decisions. If we examine this more closely, we see that certain implicit assumptions follow from this which are relevant to the discussion at hand:

1. Economic agents possess the "true" model of the economy and thus, will be able to identify the one clear path towards profit maximization.
2. As the competitive world is a world of equilibrium, a "socially responsible" decision and a "profit maximizing" decision are usually incompatible.
3. Individuals' utility functions are well-specified. Though there are notable exceptions, most mainstream economic explanations of individual choice rest upon a singular goal. As investors, individuals seek to maximize profits. In their capacity as employees, individuals seek to secure the highest wage. Customers seek to pay the lowest possible price for a given level of quality.

All of these assumptions are modernistic in the sense criticized in Chapter 2. The first assumption, that business people can identify the one clear path towards profit maximization, applies to a world of equilibrium in which plans are tightly integrated, but not to the fragmented and perpetually changing world of real markets. We have observed that a certain modernist tendency, to be found in both economics and literary theory, has been the propensity to find single, integrated unity and stasis in phenomena that are in fact multi-vocal and undergoing continuous evolution. Texts according to the New Criticism speak with one voice, even if it is ironic, and markets according to mainstream economics are in equilibrium, even if it is a balance of contrary forces of supply and demand.

If business managers only respond mechanically to what profit signals unambiguously tell them to do, if they are instantly "punished" by the market when they show any discretion, then there might not be much for the field of business ethics to talk about. In that case counseling moral virtue would amount to asking business persons to volunteer to get replaced by competitors who ignore moral issues. Within the perfect competition model, there is no room to maneuver. In this environment even the most well-meaning business owner or corporate manager is constrained by the pressures to operate at the lowest cost possible. Any redirection of investment that does not lower costs or increase sales will result in higher prices or corporate losses. Any accounting profits must be distributed to the stockholders or they will withdraw their investment in search of other opportunities in the market.

In this scenario, there is no question of how to redirect profits, because there are no long-run above-normal profits to redirect. There is no slack in how future profit opportunities are noticed, in how profit and loss statements are interpreted, in how competitors are gauged (see Lavoie 1987, 1991). If the world approximates the perfect competition model, there is little reason to even discuss the issue of moral decision-making because managers and business owners have no margin of discretion. In other words, the conclusion that managers have no social responsibility is bound up in the assumptions of equilibrium analysis. The view that profits are objective opportunities to be found, acultural and separable from the person of the entrepreneur who perceives them, suggests that there is only one correct path to achieving profit maximization and only one way to maintain one's position within the market. Any deviation from that singularly correct route will disadvantage the firm in the race to exploit the profit opportunities which lie before them.

Chapter 4 tried to suggest an alternative description of the entrepreneurial process. Profit opportunities are the outcome of an interpretive process that is highly dependent on context. Available data on demographic trends, prices of inputs and outputs, and all the other explicit information one might acquire do not speak for themselves. The data are texts that must be read within the specific cultural and economic context. Profit opportunities are not objective facts or detached things but personal achievements of culturally embedded human beings engaged in fragmented efforts of interpretation. There is no singular path to the profit maximum. A multiplicity of possible readings of the data might generate economically successful decisions. Some of these paths towards profit may include endeavors we would deem socially progressive. The choice as to which path the firm ought to take is not a purely calculative decision – it is a judgment, indeed, a moral judgment. The polysemic character of the market and the managerial discretion that is implied within that openness means that questions of morality, ethics, and values must come into play, in that except for the most mechanical of choices, all judgments contain a moral dimension.

But if there are a multitude of potentially profitable paths to market success, some of which we would agree are more socially responsible than others, then the second implicit assumption, that the socially responsible decision will usually be in conflict with the profit maximizing decision, is unfounded. The judgments business people make are usually not between clear alternatives: one profitable and some of the others socially responsible. The judgment is usually far more complex. Within the equilibrium framework, what are called "decisions" are really more like math problems to be worked out by economic agents (see Shackle 1972). There is no room for interpretation, judgment, or persuasion. But real economic life is filled with talk. McCloskey and Klamer (1994: 7–8) estimate that a full quarter of GDP is devoted to persuasion.

> Both [providing information and issuing commands] are about the machine-like side of human communication, a big and important side. The third part of economic talk is persuasion, neither information nor command. It is not any sort of machine talk. You do not persuade a machine, imagining a way to evoke loyalty to the firm with a story about your own loyalties. You feed the machine or repair it or kick it. The persuasion by contrast is a human trying to alter the behavior of another human by mere sweet talk (the Indo-European root of "sweet" is the same as that for Latin "suadeo," meaning "I persuade"). The persuasion is startlingly big... Weighted sums yield 28.2 million out of 115 million civilian employment, or about a quarter of the labor force, devoted to persuasion.

If successful business decisions are less a matter of calculus, and more a matter of judgment, perception and persuasion, however, a socially responsible business agenda is not necessarily contrary to the goal of maintaining a successful business. The existence of slack means that business decision-makers are faced with not a single, mechanically profitable optimum but a range of possibly profitable ones, a range from which more or less moral ones might be selected. Thus acting morally is fully consistent with fulfilling the contractual obligations they have to their customers, employees, and stockholders.

Of course, there is not one set of positions that represents the socially responsible but rather there is bound to be a wide range of interpretations of exactly what such responsibility entails. Noble stances on behalf of the environment may clash with noble stances on behalf of employment opportunities. Different businesses are apt to take different moral positions in the midst of this divergence. The point here is only that engaging in this public debate, or acting on behalf of social causes, are not foreign to the task of being a responsible manager of a business enterprise, but on the contrary, is an inevitable consequence of the fact that business firms are a part of the moral and political culture in which they arise.

The existence of slack means that there is room for either morally good or morally bad choices. Contrary to the impression given by some economists, the blind forces of competition alone will not necessarily yield an ethically admirable business community. As in all domains of human endeavor, virtue does not arise automatically but requires its own standard bearers.

Successful interpretations of what strategies will work in the given political culture require producers to be creative in their responses. Consider, for instance, Hanna Anderson, Inc., which supplies high quality children's clothing. The company owners Gun and Tom Denhark wanted to fix in the minds of their customers how long-lasting their products were. To any customer who returns their Hanna Anderson clothing in good used condition, the company will give a 20 percent credit towards the purchase of new Hanna Anderson clothing. The used clothes are then donated to area charities.

> The program, called Hannadowns, started as a marketing promotion intended to demonstrate the long life of the company's high-quality Swedish-made clothing. Yet the result is that thousands of needy children are now wearing the returned items that Hanna Anderson donates to worthy recipients. In 1989 and 1990, for example, more than thirty thousand of these articles of children's clothing were donated to Portland, Oregon-area shelters for battered women. (Scott and Rothman 1994: 199–200)

The strategy is a stroke of marketing genius. First, the company reaps the benefits the Hannadowns promotion generates in brand name reputation for superior quality. Second, the company generates greater returns through a price discrimination strategy. The 20 percent credit towards new clothing entices previous customers to make purchases more frequently. Third, socially minded consumers are more likely to buy Hanna Anderson products, as they have built a reputation as a company with a conscience. Given the fact that this strategy profits the company, can we call the Hannadowns promotion an act of "social responsibility?" If the answer here is "no," then we have set ourselves up for an extremely restricted view of moral action. To apply this standard consistently, we could not count philanthropic gestures as "moral" if the benefactor received the approbation and respect of his peers. Only the truly selfless and anonymous act would count as moral. Since in general, individual volunteers and philanthropists are not held to this strict interpretation of morality, it would be inconsistent to hold business to such a standard. Even more importantly, the Hanna Anderson example illustrates how business decisions are more like complex readings in which the business person negotiates the search for profits with the search for socially beneficial action.

All business decisions of any depth will have some moral content. Yet we can only see this outside of the equilibrium framework which casts the market as a closed text inhabited by passive adherents to a singularly correct path. Real decisions – those that are embedded within a cultural context of values and ethics – are not optimizing problems waiting to be calculated. Real judgments are made by creative and strategic human beings engaged in a process of interpretation. Because seeking profit opportunities is more interpretation and judgment than optimization, it leaves room for a multiplicity of profit strategies to emerge. This discretion opens the way toward socially responsible action within profitable business strategies. Entrepreneurs and social activists alike are finding that markets have the potential to effect real social change.

6.3.2   Resistant readings in the market context

Even when economists portray economic decision-making as strategic and active, the strategies pursued by consumers and producers, employees and employers are presented as singular pursuits, usually towards a financial goal. All other things remaining equal, investors are said to seek the highest return, employees the highest wage, and consumers the lowest price. Of course, economists recognize that real human beings seek to balance a variety of interests, but for the most part, the stories economists tell by way of economic theory present economic actors as driven towards a single financial goal. In these stories, there is no sense that people actively negotiate a variety of interests, some financial, others moral and ideological, in the course of their market decisions.

Some economists have attempted to incorporate nonfinancial factors within their analysis. Rosen's (1974) model of how employees self-select into positions according to various factors other than wage provides just one example of how we might modify mainstream theory to incorporate nonfinancial variables. Similarly, an environmentally aware consumer may not mind spending a little more on items produced from recycled materials because it allows him to put his convictions into practice for a relatively small cost. Analytically, this is no different than any other change in tastes and preferences. As the public alters its perceptions and priorities, many consumers may be willing to pay a premium for products which serve those new priorities. An employee may be more loyal to her firm, not because it pays her more than a competitor, but because it offers low cost day-care services on site. Even investors may seek to fulfill purposes other than profit. In fact, a niche industry of socially conscious investment firms has emerged to answer this demand in the market.

But the mainstream of economic theory is severely limited in its ability to incorporate such factors. Revenue, cost, and even utility schedules are assumed to be continuous functions, allowing the theorist to perform the calculus and derive the precise results his formalism demands. Yet moral or religious convictions are not continuous functions like well-behaved cost and revenue schedules. Values and ethics do not lend themselves to such exercises in formalism. Since financial goals are much more easily quantifiable than ideological goals, empirical studies are likely to include the former but not the latter. As most nonfinancial considerations cannot be quantified within the confines of equilibrium analysis, they tend not to get discussed at all. What we have called the formalism and quantitativism inherent within the modernistic mainstream economics framework have inhibited economists from making substantive contributions to the discussion of morality in market decisions.

In moving beyond the equilibrium model, we are not suggesting that financial considerations are unimportant or even necessarily less important than social considerations. Consumers still want low prices, employees still want high wages, and investors still want high returns. The point is that the interpretive process behind market decision-making is far more complex than mainstream economic analysis usually allows. A culturally informed economics will enable an understanding of how individuals, whether consumers, managers, employees, or stockholders, often use their market activities to live out moral and ideological convictions. As people seek to satisfy an array of criteria in their investment, consumption, and employment choices, the market responds to meet the diverse preferences present in the economy.

Yet each entrepreneur or manager will read those opportunities differently. Just as there is no single strategy towards profits, there is no single reading of how one might integrate moral and ideological commitments into business life. One business owner or manager might attend to issues of impact on the environment or on a particular group of people. Some entrepreneurs might manifest their commitments in the choice of products they produce, or in the employment and management policies they practice, others in the social causes they promote with their profits. Still other firms may build on the infrastructure their normal operations already provide. The central point is that the market can be an effective vehicle for intentional socially responsible behavior, just as it is a vehicle for unintended growth and prosperity.

6.3.3 *Doesn't business just co-opt progressive causes?*

But some cultural studies scholars would consider this sort of market response to cultural values and ideological commitments to be nothing more than a way to co-opt social criticism. So-called "socially progressive" marketing campaigns, "environmentally friendly" product lines, and new-age management techniques, some argue, all serve to further entrench, not dismantle, the hegemonic forces of capitalism (Boisvert 1997; Frank 1997a, 1997b, 1997c; Harrington 1972; Hinkle 1967; Ross 1994; Shorris 1967; White

1997). The essay entitled "Dark Age," by Thomas Frank in the book *Commodify Your Dissent* (a collection of essays from the radical journal, *The Baffler* 1997), exemplifies the kind of critique we have in mind here. He concludes on the following gloomy note:

> Even while we are happily dazed by the mall's panoply of choice, exhorted to indulge our taste for breaking rules, and deluged with all manner of useful "information," our collective mental universe is being radically circumscribed, enclosed within the tightest parameters of all time. In the third millennium there is to be no myth but the business myth, no individuality but the thirty or so professionally-accepted psychographic market niches, no diversity but the happy heteroglossia of the sitcom, no rebellion but the preprogrammed search for new kicks. Denunciation is becoming impossible: We will be able to achieve no distance from the business culture since we will no longer have a life, a history, a consciousness apart from it. It is making itself unspeakable, too big, too obvious, too vast, too horrifying, too much of a cliche to even begin addressing. A matter-of-fact disaster, as natural as the supermarket, as resistable as air. It is putting itself beyond our power of imagining because it has *become* our imagination, it has *become* our power to envision, and describe, and theorize, and resist.

This is certainly the extreme case of somebody who is alienated by the contemporary world of commercial enterprise, but there is a legitimate point here that we do not mean to trivialize. Frank charges that our present-day world, with all its material comforts, still needs further questioning, further resistance. There may be spiritual elements of our lives that we permit to atrophy while we go after the gadgets we are tempted to buy. Society needs to leave room for us to put distance between ourselves and any institution in order to find our own way in the world. If any institution, whether in government or the private sector, gets to a point where we cannot think against the grain of the dominant modes of thought, we have a problem. But what is the source of the frightening circumscriptions he finds in contemporary American society? Is it really business culture as such that limits us?

Bill Boisvert (1997: 91) not only mocks management literature that extols the values of creativity, contemplative practice, and the cultivation of a meaningful work environment, he argues that it serves to further entrench the dominance of a privileged class.

> The great challenge of business literature is thus to rejuvenate a now superfluous business class by reconstructing the mystique of the entrepreneur ... Business missionaries have renounced the old covenant of production quotas and cost-cutting; the central tenets of the entrepreneur's new catechism are "marketing," "sales," "customer service," and "flexible labor markets." But this complex of euphemisms

is really just a smokescreen concealing a retreat to capitalism's most antique and corrosive traditions of thought-control and worker oppression. For while business-lit hails progressive reforms in production, it uses the new creed of entrepreneurialism to shackle these reforms in the service of an age-old regime of futile hierarchy and mindless consumption.

If business people talk about a radical new vision, one in which business can attend to environmental and social justice issues, these cultural studies scholars are telling us to beware – those old hegemonic forces must be in play. Frank (1997a, 1997c) suggests that the process of co-optation is so complete, that there no longer exists any difference between the countercultural ideal and the dominant culture.

> Today, the beautiful countercultural idea, endorsed now by everyone from the surviving Beats to the shampoo manufacturers, is more the official doctrine of corporate America than it is a program of resistance. What we understand as "dissent" does not subvert, does not challenge, does not even question the cultural faiths of Western business. What David Reiff wrote of the revolutionary pretensions of multiculturalism is equally true of the countercultural idea: "The more one reads in academic multiculturalist journals and in business publications, and the more one contrasts the speeches of CEOs and the speeches of noted multiculturalist academics, the more one is struck by the similarities in the way they view the world." What happened is not co-optation or appropriation, but a simple and direct confluence of interests.
>
> The problem with cultural dissent in America isn't that it's been co-opted, absorbed, or ripped-off. Of course it has been all of these things. But it has proven so hopelessly susceptible to such assaults for the same reason it has become so harmless in the first place. . . It is no longer any different from the official culture it's supposed to be subverting. (Frank 1997c: 44)

In his research on the development of business culture in the advertising and men's fashion industries, Frank (1997a) argues that by the 1960s, corporate culture was already in the throws of a radical transformation that challenged bureaucracy and conformism, just as youth culture was undergoing its own cultural revolution. Though the Corporate Suits were cast as icons of rigid bureaucratic conformity, against which youth culture protested, Frank aptly points out that business desperately needed to trade the paradigms of Taylorism and hierarchy in for one which opened the way to the countercultural ideals of creativity and revolution. Business rose to the challenge, and in fact, often led the charge against the stultifying effects of traditionalism.

Yet rather than celebrating this as a victory of the countercultural movement, it is read as a sign of its defeat. After all, multiculturalism cannot have anything useful to say if CEOs can incorporate such ideas into their business practice. When the everyday practice of business is made more meaningful by the ideas of the counterculture, it is perceived as an assault on the counterculture, not an affirmation of its ideals. When they succeed in transforming business practice, the countercultural ideals themselves are deemed a failure.

The problem we find with the cultural studies work of Frank and others who argue in this vein is not that they identify many occasions of business cynically co-opting social causes for its own ends, it is that *in principle* there seems to be no other possibility. A social cause becomes suspect precisely when a business tries to promote it. There is an animus against the business world as such here that survives from the legacy of traditional Marxism. Marx thought naive the idea that the institutions of business enterprise might be reformed from within, that democratic and community values might be pursued within the system of capitalism. According to many of the leading interpreters of his message in the early part of the twentieth century (such as Lenin), what Marx offered instead of such naive reforms was the bold alternative of the revolutionary overthrow of the whole system of profit making and buying and selling, and its replacement with a centrally planned economy. We would not merely try to make for-profit business enterprises more human, we would utterly abolish them.

But what looks more naive today? Who is really ready to endorse the abolition of the system of for-profit enterprise? Marx at least had some sort of plausible hope for an alternative system that would not be based on profit and loss. Theoretical arguments and historical developments have by now extinguished those hopes. If we admit that society needs business enterprise, and if we still believe there are social causes in need of our efforts, then we ought to stop condemning those who work within the business enterprise system to achieve their ideals.

Among the traditional left, it has long been accepted wisdom that the agents of capitalism seek to appropriate the messages of social critique, but only to undermine any power it might have to make a genuine challenge to the business establishment. But recall that in responding to the traditional left, which had cast consumers of popular culture as passive victims of the capitalist machine, cultural studies recognized the potential for consumers to create resistant readings of popular culture. As discussed in Chapter 3, the cultural studies literature has passionately argued for the breakdown of the barriers between high and low culture, for the dismantling of the elitism inherent in treating some artistic preferences as "real" and other preferences as "merely commercial" and the sign of poor taste. It sees consumers of popular culture as having the potential to directly challenge and thus change the norms of the dominant culture. Yet it has not, for the most part, seen a similar role for producers, for business people themselves. To the extent that cultural studies has acknowledged the agency possessed by business people, that agency is understood to be used only to perpetuate the dominant culture.

One might ask, How can this critique escape its own challenge? If all employees even at the most enlightened businesses are really only being duped into thinking their workplaces are more democratic, does this apply as well to the academics in universities who pull down a pay check or to the editors of *The Baffler*? If all resistance is co-opted by "the system" why should we listen to even their attempts to challenge the status quo? Is there perhaps the same sort of hidden elitism behind this apparently radical message, an elitism that says, You workers at an auto plant or software company are suffering from false consciousness, but we who work in the academic world are able to see through all the lies?

Those who automatically dismiss as co-optation any efforts by business to advance social causes beg the question, what exactly is the point of social critique if not to change the lives of ordinary people engaged in ordinary pursuits? Of course we can point to examples in which corporations pay lip service to environmental and social concerns only to fend off criticism, but we must also acknowledge that many consumers (and not only academics) are very skeptical, and are unlikely to blithely accept every claim of "environmental friendliness."

We need to rethink questions of moral responsibility in the business world. We need to represent all economic actors, including business people, laborers, suppliers, and consumers as having the agency required to creatively respond to, as well as reflect the cultural context in which they act. Yet to do this we must first recognize business as a place where human beings seek and find meaning, an arena where moral responsibilities apply. We would argue that cultural studies ought to be particularly well-placed to make this move. To suggest that *all* producers either blindly or knowingly perpetuate the norms of the dominant culture poses the same problems as suggesting that all consumers passively accept the norms of the dominant culture.

Human choices made within the world of business enterprise have just as much potential to create meaning and significance for human existence as any other sort of activity, and should not be dismissed as somehow less important or less authentic simply because they are business decisions. Rather than representing the market as a place where conservative forces within society are always reproduced, we want to conceive of market activity as a sort of discursive process in which radical reinterpretations can take place. Just as a wide range of interpretations can emerge from the reading of a book or a film or a television show, the market is an open text, out of which a multitude of interpretations can be read. Though some readings may be conservative in nature, the potential for resistant and radical readings also exists.

More importantly, we have to acknowledge that sometimes the market is the most effective vehicle by which to initiate social transformation. The founders of companies such as Equal Exchange and Cafe Fair, for example, seized the opportunities in the market not only to earn profits but to correct what they saw as social injustice. Coffee growers in the developing world often sell their crop at a fraction of world market prices to the state or to government protected monopolies because there is no other alternative. These companies offer that alternative by buying directly from farm cooperatives. The crucial point is that the market is the arena in which socially motivated entrepreneurs and consumers can reveal and exercise their values and principles. To call this "mere commercialism" is to dismiss the ways in which meaning is being constructed in the market context.

We suspect that the tendency to treat social progress in the context of business as something less than real progress falls out of the unspoken bias cultural studies scholars may share with mainstream economics: that business and market activity is some kind of external force, not a forum in which people express their moral and ideological commitments. Part of this bias may come, as we have said, from the traditional left's suspicion of market activity. But the blame must be shared by economists who portray market decision-makers as if they were working out a math problem, rather than responsible human beings embedded within a complex cultural context. A cultural economics approach as outlined here might be a basis for challenging both those cultural studies scholars who have tried to rule out anything but villainy, as well as those economists who have tried to rule out ethical considerations as such from the discussion of business life. Our hope is that both cultural studies scholars and economists can come to see the openness of the market process, and to see business enterprise itself as a site of creative and active responses that have the potential to radically redefine accepted cultural norms.

Cultural studies has much to teach economics, particularly in its recognition that culture is a polysemic discursive process in which people negotiate new meanings that serve their interests and their ideals. Perhaps the main thing economists have to teach cultural studies is that the market is a critical part of this process. The market is a realm in which socially embedded individuals reinterpret constraints and creatively weave moral and ideological commitments into the world, as producers and consumers, and as employers and employees. Cultural studies needs to take its own critiques, like that which breaks down the distinction between high and low culture, more seriously. Those who characterize choice within business enterprise as incapable of creating authentic meaning and change commit the same sort of error, import the same sort of false distinction, they seek to correct elsewhere. Cultural studies needs to make the same move with the world of business as it has made with regard to popular culture – to take the decisions of human beings engaged in the practice of everyday life seriously as thoughtful expressions of their moral and ideological commitments.

7 Conclusion

The market makes a perfect totalizing enemy: it is impersonal, has no particular location and legitimates itself through a myriad of democratic practices of buying and selling. . . . The problem is that . . . the market is a democratic institution aggregating the decisions of whomever participates in it. When all is said and done, complaints about the market are nothing but complaints about the people themselves. . .

Paul Piccone (1994: 202)

Communal freedom is freedom that – through the institutions and practices of a society, through the self-understanding, concern, and habits of its citizens – has become a common *objective*. Negative freedom changes its character when it becomes a common concern. For then it is not only our own freedom we want but a maximum of self-determination for each individual and collective. Such a common – and commonly recognized – space of self-determination can exist, however, only if a space of public freedom is institutionalized in which *we*, constrained by the demands of rationality and justice, collectively, i.e., in the medium of public debate and by "acting in concert,"exert our right of self-determination as a *political* right.

Albrecht Wellmer (1991: 249)

Our culture is itself split in a way that has kept us from understanding the cultural elements of the economy. It is in the humanities where scholars have cultivated the understanding of culture, but economics has wanted to see itself as siding with the "sciences" side of the two cultures. Economics has, over the years, learned important things about how the economy works, what is involved in business decision-making, and what underlies economic development, but what it knows remains in a very abstract language and seems to come rarely into ethnographic contact with culture, with the empirical reality of the meanings of everyday life. Long-standing ideological divisions between left and right reinforce the distance between economists and cultural studies scholars.

Though coming from opposite sides of the methodological and ideological spectra, economics and cultural studies can be seen as highly complementary with one another. Economics needs the skills in "reading" cultural texts and the ethnographic contact that cultural studies has, and cultural studies needs the understanding of market institutions and what they need to work, that economics has. There are strands in each of these literatures – for example, what Willis and the popular culture movement say about cultural markets, what the critical theory movement led by such scholars as Habermas and Wellmer says about the public sphere, and what economics has to say about comparative advantage and entrepreneurship – that could be woven into a culturally informed economics.

If we grant that economics needs to pay more attention to the role of culture and that cultural studies needs to recognize that markets are cultural phenomena, we need to ask specifically how culture and markets shape one another. How, for example, should we try to ask the question about the relationship between culture and economic prosperity? One common approach, which we have called cultural nationalism, tries to operate on such a grand scale – summarizing an entire nation's set of cultural values, and comparing them with those of other nations – that it has had little useful to say about any one value or any one culture. Cultural nationalism, absent as it is of influence from either cultural studies or economics, shows why, with all their warts, we need to use what has been painstakingly developed in those disciplines.

A more promising approach goes for ethnographic contact instead of statistical scope. It combines the anthropological and literary research methods of cultural studies with an appreciation from economic theory about what kinds of activities are conducive to economic development. Studying a small number of cases up close seems to show us more about the complex interplay that takes place between cultural and market processes than larger statistical studies have been able to show. A survey of some of the writings on Japanese, American, and Chinese entrepreneurship suggests that while certain abstract elements of creativity are common, the sort of behavior each culture appropriately calls entrepreneurial is entirely different in each cultural milieu. Ethnographic research of this kind, as has been conducted by the Institute for the Study of Economic Culture, has begun to show us a side of our economy that the traditional empirical methods of economists have been unable to see. (See also Chamlee 1994; Chamlee-Wright 1997; Lavoie 1990b.) Such research strongly suggests that culture, in the general sense of a set of widely shared values and beliefs, is an important influence over economic prosperity. For example, the prevalence of certain values in a cultural context can add up to a larger degree of entrepreneurialism, and a more vibrant enterprising spirit.

And culture in the narrower sense of the popular arts is, in turn, one of the crucial arenas in which such values are cultivated. The portrayal of heroic and villainous characters in stories we encounter in popular culture is where we pick up images of the kind of person we aspire to be, and the kind we distrust. Looking at the way business life is usually represented in contemporary American television and cinema, it is not surprising that the notion of the creative business entrepreneur is not one of the strongest heroic images in our systems of belief.

Markets and business life are not so much disliked because critics have shown any specific defects in how they work. They are disliked because they are perceived as ugly, as dead, rationalistic, calculating machines, in contrast to our living culture. Economics has pretty much won in making the argument that markets work more efficiently than government ownership or regulation. What it has failed to do is show that they are beautiful, that they are human. When business decision-making is treated as an amoral problem of calculation, not as an occasion for making moral choices, it should not be surprising that it is left out of our culture's vision of the human world and depicted as an external force. But when markets and business enterprise are no longer conceived of as impersonal mechanisms externally working their cold logic *upon* our choices, but as meaningful expressions *of* our choices, when business is seen to constitute a significant portion of society's cultural life, there is a better chance that our culture will value them at their worth.

Business persons and economists can hope that a better understanding of markets and business life on the part of students of culture might improve the odds of encountering the occasional story that has entrepreneurial heroes and heroines. If we come to see that markets are not some sort of soul-less mechanism, but an integral part of our culture, are filled with the drama of human creativity and error, of moral leadership and of ethical disgrace, that they are essentially reflections of who we are, we might begin to recover our culture's entrepreneurial stories and images. We might begin to see some celebration by our civilization of the spirit of enterprise that has made it flourish.

Bibliography

Acton, Thomas A. 1990. "Ethnicity and Religion in the Development of Family Capitalism: Seui-Seung-Yahn Immigrants from Hong Kong to Scotland." In S.R. Clegg and S.G. Redding *et. al.*, eds. *Capitalism in Contrasting Cultures*. New York: Walter de Gruyter.

Addleson, Mark 1995. *Equilibrium Versus Understanding: Towards the Restoration of Economics as Social Theory*. New York: Routledge.

Alchian, Armen and Demsetz, Harold 1973. "The Property Rights Paradigm." *Journal of Economic History*, 331.

Amariglio, Jack 1990. "Economics as a Postmodern Discourse." In Warren J. Samuels, ed. *Economics as Discourse*. Boston: Kluwer Academic Publishers.

Anderson, B.L. and Latham, A.J.H., eds. 1986. *The Market in History*. London: Croom Helm.

Anderson, Martin 1992. *Impostors in the Temple*. New York: Simon and Schuster.

Arendt, Hannah 1958. *The Human Condition*. Chicago: University of Chicago Press.

—— [1961] 1968. *Between Past and Future: Eight Exercises in Political Thought*. New York: Penguin.

Ashcraft, Richard 1986. *Revolutionary Politics and Locke's Two Treatises of Government*. Princeton, NJ: Princeton University Press.

Ayittey, George 1991. *Indigenous African Institutions*. New York: Transnational Publishers, Inc.

Baechler, Jean 1975. *The Origins of Capitalism*. Oxford: Basil Blackwell.

Bauer, P.T. 1954. *West African Trade: A Study of Competition, Oligopoly, and Monopoly in a Changing Economy*. Cambridge: Cambridge University Press.

—— 1957. *The Economics of Underdeveloped Countries*. Chicago: University of Chicago Press.

—— 1971. *Dissent on Development*. Cambridge, MA: Harvard University Press.

—— 1984. *Reality and Rhetoric: Studies in the Economics of Development*. London: Weidenfeld & Nicolson.

Beiner, Ronald 1993. "Richard Rorty's Liberalism." *Critical Review*, 7: 1 15–31.

Beito, David T. 1990. "Mutual Aid for Social Welfare: The Case of American Fraternal Societies." *Critical Review*, 4: 4 709–36.

Benhabib, Seyla 1992. "Models of Public Space: Hannah Arendt, the Liberal Tradition, and Jürgen Habermas." In Craig Calhoun, ed. *Habermas and the Public Sphere*. Cambridge, MA: The MIT Press: 73–98.

Benhabib, Seyla and Dallmayr, Fred, eds. 1990. *The Communicative Ethics Controversy*. Cambridge, Mass.: MIT Press.

Bennett, William J. 1994. *The Index of Leading Cultural Indicators: Facts and Figures on the State of American Society*. New York: Simon& Schuster.

Benton, Raymond, Jr. 1990. "A Hermeneutic Approach to Economics: If Economics is Not Science, and If It Is Not Merely Mathematics, Then What Could It Be?." In Warren J. Samuels, ed. *Economics as Discourse*. Boston: Kluwer Academic Publishers.

Berger, Brigitte, ed. 1991. *The Culture of Entrepreneurship*. San Francisco: Institute for Contemporary Studies.

Berger, Peter L. 1986. *The Capitalist Revolution*. New York: Basic Books.

Berger, Peter L. and Hsiao, H.M., eds. 1988. *In Search of an East Asian Development Model*. New Brunswick: Transaction Books.

Berger, Peter L. and Luckmann, Thomas 1966. *The Social Construction of Reality: A Treatise in the Sociology of Knowledge*. New York: Doubleday.

Bernstein, Irving 1985. *A Caring Society: The New Deal, the Worker, and the Great Depression*. Boston: Houghton Mifflin.

Biggart, Nicole Woolsey 1990. "Charismatic Capitalism: Direct Selling Organizations in the USA and Asia." In S.R. Clegg and S.G. Redding, eds. *Capitalism in Contrasting Cultures*. New York: Walter de Gruyter.

Black, Anthony 1984. *Guilds and Civil Society in European Political Thought from the Twentieth Century to the Present*. Ithaca: Cornell University Press.

Boettke, Peter J., ed. 1994. *The Collapse of Development Planning*. New York: NYU Press.

Boisvert, Bill 1997. "Apostles of the New Entrepreneur: Business Books and the Management Crisis." In Thomas Frank and Matt Weiland, eds. *Commodify Your Dissent: Salvos from The Baffler*. New York: W.W. Norton: 81–9.

Bourdieu, Pierre 1977. "The Economics of Linguistic Exchange." *Social Science Information*, 16: 645–88.

—— [1979] 1984. *Distinction: A Social Critique of the Judgment of Taste*. Trans. Richard Nice. Cambridge, MA: Harvard University Press.

—— 1993. *The Field of Cultural Production: Essays on Art and Literature*. New York: Columbia University Press.

Brantlinger, Patrick 1990. *Crusoe's Footprints: Cultural Studies in Britain and America*. London: Routledge.

Burczak, Theodore 1996. "Socialism After Hayek." *Rethinking Marxism*, 9 (3) 1–18.

Calhoun, Craig, ed. 1992. *Habermas and the Public Sphere*. Cambridge, MA: The MIT Press.

Chamlee, Emily 1994. "Indigenous African Institutions." *The Cato Journal*, 131: 79–99.

Chamlee-Wright, Emily 1997. *The Cultural Foundations of Economic Development: Urban Female Entrepreneurship in Ghana*. New York: Routledge.

Clark, Gracia 1994. *Onions Are My Husband: Survival and Accumulation by West African Market Women*. Chicago: University of Chicago Press.

Clark, John Bates 1899 [1928]. *The Distribution of Wealth: A Theory of Wages, Interest, and Profits*. New York: Macmillan.

Clegg, Stewart R. and Redding, S. Gordon, eds. 1990. *Capitalism in Contrasting Cultures*. New York: Walter de Gruyter.

Coase, Ronald H. 1959. "The Federal Communications Commission." *Journal of Law and Economics*, 2 October.

—— 1974. "The Lighthouse in Economics." *Journal of Law and Economics*, Oct.

Cornell, Stephen and Kalt, Joseph 1995. "Constitutional Rule Among the Sioux and Apache." *Economic Inquiry*, 333: 402–26.

Cowen, Tyler 1998. *In Praise of Commercial Culture*. Cambridge, MA: Harvard University Press.

Cullenberg, S. 1992. "Socialism's Burden: Toward a 'Thin' Definition of Socialism." *Rethinking Marxism*, 5 (2): 64–83.

Danley, John R. 1994. *The Role of the Modern Corporation in a Free Society*. Notre Dame: University of Notre Dame Press.

Davis, Robert Con and Schleiffer, Ronald, eds. 1989. *Contemporary Literary Criticism: Literary and Cultural Studies*. New York: Longman.

de Certeau, Michel 1984. "Reading as Poaching." *The Practice of Everyday Life*. trans. Steven F. Rendall, Berkeley: University of California Press.

De Soto, Hernando 1988. *The Other Path*. New York: Harper & Row.

D'Souza, Dinesh 1991. *Illiberal Education: The Politics of Race and Sex on Campus*. New York: Free Press.

Denzau, Arthur and North, Douglass C. 1994. "Shared Mental Models: Ideologies and Institutions." *Kyklos*, 47: 3–30.

diZerega, Gus 1989. "Democracy as a Spontaneous Order." *Critical Review*, 3: 2 206–40.

Douglas, Mary and Isherwood, Baron 1979. *The World of Goods: Towards an Anthropology of Consumption*. London: Allen Lane.

During, Simon 1993a. "Introduction." In Simon During, ed. *The Cultural Studies Reader*. New York: Routledge.

—— ed. 1993b. *The Cultural Studies Reader*. New York: Routledge.

Ebeling, Richard M. 1986. "Toward a Hermeneutical Economics: Expectations, Prices, and the Role of Interpretation in a Theory of the Market Process." In Kirzner, ed. *Subjectivism, Intelligibility, and Economic Understanding: Essays in Honor of Ludwig M. Lachmann on his Eightieth Birthday*. New York: New York University Press.

Eco, Umberto [1972] 1980. "Towards a Semiotic Inquiry into the TV Message." In J. Corner and J. Hawthorn, eds. *Communication Studies: An Introductory Reader*. London: Arnold.

Eichner, Alfred S., ed. 1978. *A Guide to Post-Keynesian Economics*. New York: M.E. Sharpe.

Ensminger, Jean 1992. *Making a Market: The Institutional Transformation of an African Society*. Cambridge: Cambridge University Press.

Fiske, John 1989. *Television Culture*. London: Routledge.

—— 1996. "British Cultural Studies and Television." In John Storey, ed. *What is Cultural Studies? A Reader*. London: Arnold: 125–46.

Fong, Pang Eng 1988. "The Distinctive Features of Two City-States' Development: Hong Kong and Singapore." In B. Berger, ed. *The Culture of Entrepreneurship*. San Francisco: Institute for Contemporary Studies Press.

Foucault, Michel [1969] 1972. *The Archaeology of Knowledge*. New York: Pantheon.

Fox, Richard Wightman and Lears, T.J. Jackson 1993. *The Power of Culture: Critical Essays in American History*. Chicago: University of Chicago Press.

Frank, Thomas 1997a. *The Conquest of Cool: Business Culture, Counterculture, and the Rise of Hip Consumerism*. Chicago: University of Chicago Press.

—— 1997b. "Opening Salvo: The New Gilded Age." In Thomas Frank and Matt Weiland eds. *Commodify Your Dissent: Salvos from The Baffler*. New York: W.W. Norton: 23–8.

—— 1997c. "Why Johnny Can't Dissent." In Thomas Frank and Matt Weiland eds. *Commodify Your Dissent: Salvos from The Baffler.* New York: W.W. Norton: 31–45.

Frank, Thomas and Weiland, Matt eds. 1997. *Commodify Your Dissent: Salvos from The Baffler.* New York: W.W. Norton.

Friedman, Milton 1962. *Capitalism and Freedom.* Chicago: University of Chicago Press.

—— 1980. *Free To Choose.* New York: Harcourt Brace Jovanovich.

—— [1970] 1987. "The Social Responsibility of Business." *The Essence of Friedman.* Stanford: Hoover Institution Press.

Fukuyama, Francis 1995. *Trust: The Social Virtues and the Creation of Prosperity.* New York: The Free Press.

Gadamer, Hans-Georg [1960] 1989. *Truth and Method,* revised. Translated by J. Weinsheimer and D. Marshall. New York: Crossroad.

Gastil, John 1993. *Democracy in Small Groups: Participation, Decision Making, and Communication.* Philadelphia, PA: New Society Publishers.

Geertz, Clifford 1973. *The Interpretation of Cultures.* New York: Basic Books.

Genovese, Eugene 1994. *The Southern Tradition.* Cambridge, MA: Harvard University Press.

Geraghty, Christine 1991. *Women and Soap Opera: A Study of Prime Time Soaps.* Cambridge, England: Polity Press.

Gerbner, George 1984. "Political Functions of Television Viewing." In Gabrielle Melischek, K. Rosengarten, and J. Stappers, eds. *Cultural Indicators: An International Symposium.* Vienna: Austrian Academy of Sciences: 329–43.

Ghosh, P. K. 1984. *Third World Development: A Basic Needs Approach.* Westport: Greenwood Press.

Gitlin, Todd 1995. "The Rise of 'Identity Politics': An Examination and a Critique." In Michael Berube and Cary Nelson, eds. *Higher Education Under Fire: Politics, Economics, and the Crisis of the Humanities.* New York: Routledge: 308–25.

Grossberg, Lawrence 1992. "The In-Difference of Television, or Mapping TV's Popular Affective Economy." *Screen,* 2(8): 28–45.

Grossberg, Lawrence, Nelson, Cary, and Treichler, Paula, eds. 1992. *Cultural Studies.* New York: Routledge.

Gudeman, Stephen 1986. *Economics as Culture: Models and Metaphors of Livelihood.* London: Routledge.

Gwartney, James, Lawson, Robert and Block, Walter 1996. *Economic Freedom of the World, 1975–1995.* Vancouver: Frasier Instute.

Habermas, Jürgen [1962] 1989. *The Structural Transformation of the Public Sphere: An Inquiry into a Category of Bourgeois Society.* Cambridge, MA: The MIT Press.

—— 1992a. "Further Reflections on the Public Sphere." In Craig Calhoun, ed. *Habermas and the Public Sphere.* Cambridge, MA: The MIT Press: 421–61.

—— 1992b. "Concluding Remarks." In Craig Calhoun, ed. *Habermas and the Public Sphere.* Cambridge, MA: The MIT Press: 462–79.

Hall, Stuart 1980. "Encoding/Decoding." In S. Hall, D. Hobson, A. Lowe, and P. Willis, eds. *Culture, Media, Language.* London: Hutchinson: 128–39.

Harrington, Michael 1972. "We Few, We Happy Few, We Bohemians." *Esquire,* August: 164, 99.

Harrison, Lawrence E. 1992. *Who Prospers? How Cultural Values Shape Economic and Political Success.* New York: Basic Books.

Harriss, J., Hunter, J., and Lewis, C.M., eds. 1995. *The New Institutional Economics and Third World Development*. London: Routledge.

Havel, Vaclav 1992. *Summer Meditations*. Translated by Paul Wilson. New York: Alfred A. Knopf.

Hayek, F.A. 1942. "The Facts of the Social Sciences." In Hayek, *Individualism and Economic Order*. Chicago: University of Chicago Press, 1948.

—— 1948. *Individualism and Economic Order*. Chicago: University of Chicago Press.

—— ed. 1954. *Capitalism and the Historians*. Chicago: University of Chicago Press.

—— 1955. *The Counter-Revolution of Science*. London: Free Press of Glencoe.

—— 1979. "Three Sources of Human Values." In F.A. Hayek. *Law, Legislation and Liberty: A New Statement of the Liberal Principles of Justice and Political Economy, vol. III, The Political Order of a Free People*. London: Routledge & Kegan Paul.

—— 1988. *The Fatal Conceit: The Errors of Socialism*. London: Routledge.

Hayward, Jennifer 1997. *Consuming Pleasures: Active Audiences and Serial Fictions from Dickens to Soap Opera*. Lexington: University Press of Kentucky.

Hazlitt, Henry 1964. *The Foundations of Morality*. New York: D. Van Nostrand Co.

Hill, Polly 1963. *The Migrant Cocoa Farmers in Southern Ghana: A Study in Rural Capitalism*. Cambridge: Cambridge University Press.

—— 1986. *Development Economics on Trial: The Anthropological Case for a Prosecution*. New York: Cambridge University Press.

Hinkle, Warren 1967. "A Social History of the Hippies." *Ramparts*, March, reprinted in Gerry Howard, ed. 1991. *The Sixties: Art, Politics and Media of Our Most Explosive Decade*. New York: Paragon House: 226.

Hobson, D. 1982. *Crossroads: The Drama of a Soap Opera*. London: Methuen.

Hodge, Robert and Tripp, David 1986. *Children and Television: A Semiotic Approach*. Cambridge: Polity Press.

Hodgson, Geoffrey M. 1988. *Economics and Institutions: A Manifesto for Modern Institutional Economics*. Philadelphia: University of Pennsylvania Press.

Hoggart, Richard 1957. *The Uses of Literacy*. Harmondsworth: Penguin.

Holmes, Steven 1995. *Passions and Constraints: On the Theory of Liberal Democracy*. Chicago: University of Chicago Press.

Horkheimer, Max and Adorno, Theodor [1947] 1988. *Dialectic of Enlightenment*. Trans. John Cummings. New York: Continuum.

Inglehart, Ronald 1990. *Culture Shift in Advanced Industrial Society*. Princeton: Princeton University Press.

Jackall, Robert 1988. *Moral Mazes: The World of Corporate Managers*. New York: Oxford University Press.

Jacobs, Mark 1994. Brochure on the Cultural Studies Ph.D program at George Mason University.

Jay, Gregory and Graff, Gerald 1995. "A Critique of Critical Pedagogy." In Michael Berube and Cary Nelson, eds. *Higher Education Under Fire: Politics, Economics, and the Crisis of the Humanities*. New York: Routledge: 201–13.

Jenkins, Henry 1992. *Textual Poachers: Television Fans and Participatory Culture*: London: Routledge.

Johnson, Gregory R. 1990. "Hermeneutics: A Protreptic" *Critical Review*, 4: 1–2 173–211.

Kahn, H. 1979. *World Economic Development: 1979 and Beyond*. London: Croom Helm.

Kandell, Jonathan 1988. *La Capital: The Biography of Mexico City*. New York: Random House.

Katz, E. and Liebes, T. 1984. "Once Upon a Time in Dallas." *Intermedia*, 12, 3 28–32.

Kirzner, Israel M. 1963. *Market Theory and the Price System*. Princeton, NJ: D. Van Nostrand.

—— 1973. *Competition and Entrepreneurship*. Chicago: University of Chicago Press.

—— 1979. *Perception, Opportunity, and Profit: Studies in the Theory of Entrepreneurship*. Chicago: University of Chicago Press.

—— 1985. *Discovery and the Capitalist Process*. Chicago: University of Chicago Press.

—— 1992. *The Meaning of Market Process: Essays in the Development of Modern Austrian Economics*. New York: Routledge.

— ed. 1986. *Subjectivism, Intelligibility, and Economic Understanding: Essays in Honor of Ludwig M. Lachmann on his Eightieth Birthday*. New York: New York University Press.

Klamer, Arjo 1983. *Conversations with Economists*. Totowa, NJ: Rowman & Allanheld.

Kotkin, Joel 1992. *Tribes: How Race, Religion, and Identity Determine Success in the New Global Economy*. New York: Random House.

Kreutzner, Gabriele and Warth, Eva-Marie 1994. "Gendered Meanings: Soap Operas and Female Viewers." In Borchers *et al.*, eds. *Never Ending Stories: American Soap Operas and the Cultural Production of Meaning*. Trier: Wissenschaftlichter Verlag Trier: 195–215.

Lachmann, Ludwig M. 1971. *The Legacy of Max Weber*. Berkeley: Glendessary Press.

—— 1991. "Austrian Economics: a Hermeneutic Approach." In Don Lavoie, ed. *Economics and Hermeneutics*. London: Routledge.

—— 1994. *Expectations and the Meaning of Institutions: Essays in Economics by Ludwig Lachmann*. London: Routledge.

Landa, Janet 1991. "Culture and Entrepreneurship in Less-Developed Countries: Ethnic Trading Networks as Economic Organizations." In B. Berger, ed. *The Culture of Entrepreneurship*, San Francisco: Institute for Contemporary Studies Press.

Landow, George P. 1992. *Hypertext: The Convergence of Contemporary Critical Theory and Technology*. Baltimore: Johns Hopkins University Press.

Lanham, Richard A. 1995. *The Electronic Word: Democracy, Technology, and the Arts*. Chicago: University of Chicago Press.

Lavoie, Don 1985. *National Economic Planning: What Is Left?* Cambridge, Mass.: Ballinger.

—— 1987. "The Accounting of Interpretations and the Interpretation of Accounts: The Communicative Function of 'The Language of Business'." *Accounting, Organizations and Society*, 12: 579–604.

—— 1990a. "Computation, Incentives, and Discovery: The Cognitive Function of Markets in Market-Socialism." *The Annals of the American Academy of Political and Social Science*, 507: 72–9.

—— 1990b. "Hermeneutics, Subjectivity, and the Lester/Machlup Debate: Toward a More Anthropological Approach to Empirical Economics." In Warren Samuels, ed. *Economics As Discourse*. Boston: Kluwer Academic Publishing.

—— 1990c. "Understanding Differently: Hermeneutics and the Spontaneous Order of Communicative Processes." *History of Political Economy*. Annual Supplement to Vol. 22, 359–77.

—— 1990d. "Introduction to F.A. Hayek's Theory of Cultural Evolution: Market

and Cultural Processes As Spontaneous Orders." *Cultural Dynamics*, 3: 1 1–9.
—— 1991. "The Discovery and Interpretation of Profit Opportunities: Culture and the Kirznerian Entrepreneur." In Brigitte Berger, ed. *The Culture of Entrepreneurship*. San Francisco: Institute for Contemporary Studies.
—— 1992. "*Glasnost* and the Knowledge Problem: Rethinking Economic Democracy." *Cato Journal*, 11, 3 Winter, 435–55.
—— 1993. "Democracy, Markets, and the Legal Order: Notes on the Nature of Politics in a Radically Liberal Society." In E. Paul, F D. Miller, and J. Paul, eds. *Liberalism and the Economic Order*. New York: Cambridge University Press, 103–20; also published in *Social Philosophy and Policy*, 10: 2.
—— 1995. "The 'Objectivity' of Scholarship and the Ideal of the University." *Advances in Austrian Economics*, 2B: 371–403.
Leitch, Vincent B. 1988. *American Literary Criticism From the Thirties to the Eighties*. New York: Columbia University Press.
Lichter, S. Robert, Lichter, Linda, and Amundson, Daniel 1997. "Does Hollywood Hate Business or Money?" *Journal of Communication*, 47, 1.
Lichter, S. Robert, Lichter, Linda, and Rothman, Stanley 1991. *Watching America*. New York: Prentice Hall Press.
Little, Kenneth 1965. *West African Urbanization: A Study of Voluntary Associations in Social Change*. Cambridge: Cambridge University Press.
—— 1973. *African Women in Towns*. Cambridge: Cambridge University Press.
London, Herbert 1987. "What TV Drama is Teaching Our Children." *New York Times*, August 23.
MacCabe, C. 1976. "Theory and Film: Principles of Realism and Pleasure." *Screen* 17: 7–27.
McCarthy, Thomas 1992. "Practical Discourse: On the Relation of Morality to Politics." In Craig Calhoun, ed. *Habermas and the Public Sphere*. Cambridge, MA: The MIT Press: 51–72.
McCloskey, D.N. 1985. *The Rhetoric of Economics*. Madison, Wisconsin: University of Wisconsin Press.
—— 1990. *If You're So Smart: The Narrative of Economic Expertise*. Chicago: University of Chicago Press.
—— 1991. "Storytelling in Economics." In Don Lavoie, ed. *Economics and Hermeneutics*. London: Routledge: 61–75.
—— 1997. *The Vices of Economists: The Virtues of the Bourgeoisie*. Amsterdam: University of Amsterdam Press.
McCloskey, D.N. and Klamer, A. 1994. "One Quarter of GDP is Persuasion." Keynote Address for the Southern Economic Association.
Madison, G.B. 1988. "Postmodern Philosophy?" *Critical Review*, 2, 2–3: 166–82.
—— 1989. "Hayek and the Interpretive Turn." *Critical Review*, 3, 2: 169–85.
—— 1990a. "How Individualistic is Methodological Individualism?" *Critical Review*, 4, 1–2: 41–60.
—— 1990b. "Between Theory and Practice: Hayek on the Logic of Cultural Dynamics." *Cultural Dynamics*, 3, 1: 84–112.
—— 1991a. "The Practice of Theory, the Theory of Practice." *Critical Review*, 5, 2: 179–202.
—— 1991b. "Getting Beyond Objectivism: The Philosophical Hermeneutics of Gadamer and Ricoeur." In Don Lavoie, ed. *Economics and Hermeneutics*. London: Routledge: 34–58.

Makaryk, Irena R. 1993. *Encyclopedia of Contemporary Literary Theory: Approaches, Scholars, Terms*. Toronto: University of Toronto Press.

Makower, Joel 1994. *Beyond the Bottom Line: Putting Social Responsibility to Work for Your Business and the World*. New York: Simon & Schuster.

Martin, David 1990. *Tongues of Fire*. Oxford: Basil Blackwell.

Massing, H. 1987. "Decoding *Dallas*: Comparing American and German Viewers." In A. Berger, ed. *Television and Society*. New Brunswick: Transaction Books.

Minogue, Kenneth 1989. "Can Radicalism Survive Michel Foucault?" *Critical Review*, 3, 1: 138–54.

Mises, Ludwig von [1949] 1966. *Human Action: A Treatise on Economics*, 3rd edition, revised. Chicago: Henry Regnery Company.

Modleski, Tania 1984. *Loving with a Vengeance: Mass Produced Fantasies for Women*. London: Methuen.

Moog, Clodomir Vianna 1964. *Bandeirantes e Pioneiros*. Rio de Janeiro: Editora Civilizacao Brasileira.

Moon, Parker T. 1926. *Imperialism and World Politics*. New York: Macmillan.

Moores, Shaun 1992. "Texts, Readers, and Contexts of Reading." In Paddy Scannell, Philip Schlesinger and Colin Sparks, eds. *Culture and Power: A Media, Culture and Society Reader*. London: Sage Publications: 137–57.

—— 1993. *Interpreting Audiences: The Ethnography of Media Consumption*. London: Sage Publications.

Morley, David 1980. *Nationwide Audience: Structure and Decoding*. London: British Film Institute.

Munch, Richard and Smelser, Neil J. 1992. *Theory of Culture*. Berkeley: University of California Press.

Munkata, Iwao 1988. "The Distinctive Features of Japanese Development: Basic Cultural Patterns and Politico-Economic Processes." In B. Berger, ed. *The Culture of Entrepreneurship*. San Francisco: Institute for Contemporary Studies Press.

Murakami, Y. 1986. "Technology in Transition: Two Perspectives on Industrial Policy." In H. Patrick and L. Meissner, eds. *Japan's High Technology Industries: Lessons and Limitation of Industrial Policy*. Seattle: University of Washington Press.

Murphy, James Bernard 1995. "Rational Choice Theory as Social Physics." *Critical Review*, 9, 1–2: 155–74.

Neaman, Elliot Yale 1988. "Liberalism and Post-Modern Hermeneutics." *Critical Review*, 2, 2–3: 149–65.

North, Douglass C. 1989. "Institutions and Economic Growth: An Historical Introduction." *World Development*, 179: 1319–32.

—— 1990. *Institutions, Institutional Change, and Economic Performance*. Cambridge: Cambridge University Press.

—— 1994. "Economic Performance Through Time." *The American Economic Review*, 843: 359–68.

O'Driscoll, Gerald P., Jr. and Rizzo, M. J. 1985. *The Economics of Time and Ignorance*. New York: Columbia University Press.

Oliner, Pearl M. and Oliner, Samuel P. 1995. *Toward a Caring Society: Ideas into Action*. London: Praeger.

Palmer, Tom G. 1991a. "The Hermeneutical View of Freedom: Implications of Gadamerian Understanding for Economic Policy." In Don Lavoie, ed. *Economics and Hermeneutics*. London: Routledge.

—— 1991b. "Gadamer's Hermeneutics and Social Theory." *Critical Review*, 1, 3: 91–108.

Pampel, Fred 1994. "Marketing and Movies." *American Demographics*, 16, 3, March: 48–9, 52–4.

Parsons, Stephen D. 1991. "Time, Expectations, and Subjectivism: Prolegomena to a Dynamic Economics." *Cambridge Journal of Economics*, 15: 405–23.

Piccone, Paul 1994. "From the New Left to the New Populism." *Telos*, 101 Fall: 173–208.

Pinkney, Tony 1991. "Raymond Williams" entry in Tom Bottomore, ed. *A Dictionary of Marxist Thought*, second edition. Cambridge, MA: Harvard University Press.

Prendergast, Christopher 1986. "Alfred Schütz and the Austrian School of Economics." *American Journal of Sociology*, 92, 1 July: 1–26.

Prychitko, David L. 1990a. "Toward an Interpretive Economics: Some Hermeneutic Issues." *Methodus*, 2, 2 Dec.: 69–71.

—— 1990b. "The Welfare State: What is Left?" *Critical Review*, 4, 4: 619–32.

Putnam, Robert D. 1993. "The Prosperous Community: Social Capital and Public Life." *The American Prospect*, Spring 13: 35–41.

—— 1995. "Bowling Alone: America's Declining Social Capital." *Journal of Democracy*, 61: 65–78.

—— 1996. "The Strange Disappearance of Civic America." *The American Prospect*, Winter 24: 34–48.

Putnam, Robert D., Leonardi, R., Nanetti, R. and Pavancello, F. 1983. "Explaining Institutional Success: The Case of Italian Regional Government." *The American Political Science Review*, 77: 55–74.

Rabinow, Paul and Sullivan, W.M., eds. 1987. *Interpretive Social Science: A Second Look*. Berkeley, CA: University of California Press.

Radway, Janice A. 1984. *Reading the Romance: Women, Patriarchy, and Popular Literature*. Chapel Hill: University of North Carolina Press.

Redding, S. Gordon 1990. *The Spirit of Chinese Capitalism*. New York: Walter de Gruyter.

Reed, John Shelton 1986. *The Enduring South*. Chapel Hill: University of North Carolina Press.

—— 1995. *Kicking Back*. St. Louis: University of Missouri Press.

Ricoeur, Paul 1971. "The Model of the Text: Meaningful Action Considered As a Text." *Social Research*, 38: 3 Autumn 529–62. Republished in Paul Ricoeur, *Hermeneutics and the Human Sciences*. Edited and translated by J. B. Thompson. New York: Cambridge University Press: 197–221.

Robben, Antonius C.G.M. 1989. *Sons of the Sea Goddess: Economic Practice and Discursive Conflict in Brazil*. New York: Columbia Univ. Press.

Robertson, Claire 1984. *Sharing the Same Bowl: A Socioeconomic History of Women and Class in Accra*. Bloomington: Indiana University Press.

Rosen, Sherwin 1974. "Hedonic Prices and Implicit Markets: Product Differentiation in Pure Competition." *Journal of Political Economy*, January.

Rosenberg, Nathan and Birdzell, L.E., Jr. 1986. *How the West Grew Rich: The Economic Transformation of the Industrial World*. New York: Basic Books.

Ross, Andrew 1994. *The Chicago Gangster Theory of Life: Nature's Debt to Society*. London: Verso.

Sahlins, Marshall 1976. *Culture and Practical Reason*. Chicago: University of Chicago Press.

Said, Edward W. 1983. *The World, the Text, and the Critic*. Cambridge, MA: Harvard University Press.

—— 1993. "Expanding Humanism: An Interview." In Mark Edmundson, ed. *Wild Orchids and Trotsky: Messages from American Universities*. New York: Penguin: 101–23.

Samuels, Warren, ed. 1990. *Economics As Discourse*. Boston: Kluwer Academic Publishing.

Sarup, Madan 1989. *An Introductory Guide to Post-Structuralism and Postmodernism*. Athens: University of Georgia Press.

Schiff, S. 1985. "What Dynasty Says about America." *Vanity Fair*, 4712: 64–7.

Schrag, Calvin O. 1991. "Reconstructing Reason in the Aftermath of Deconstruction." *Critical Review*, 5, 2: 247–60.

Sciabarra, Chris 1987. "The Crisis of Libertarian Dualism." *Critical Review*, 1, 4: 86–99.

Scott, Mary and Rothman, Howard 1994. *Companies with a Conscience*. New York: Carol Publishing Group.

Selden, Raman 1989. *A Reader's Guide to Contemporary Literary Theory*. Lexington: University Press of Kentucky.

Sethi, S. Prakash and Steidlmeier, Paul 1991. *Up Against the Corporate Wall*. Englewood Cliffs, NJ: Prentice-Hall.

Shackle, G.L.S. 1972. *Epistemics and Economics: A Critique of Economic Doctrines*. Cambridge: Cambridge University Press.

Shorris, Earl 1967. "Love is Dead." *New York Times Magazine*, October 29: 114.

Smith, Adam [1759] 1984. *The Theory of Moral Sentiments*. Edited by D. D. Raphael and A. L. MacFie. Indianapolis: Liberty Fund.

Smith, Barbara Herrnstein 1988. *Contingencies of Value: Alternative Perspectives for Critical Theory*. Cambridge, MA: Harvard University Press.

Solomon, Robert 1994. *The New World of Business: Ethics and Free Enterprise in the Global 1990s*. Lanham, MD: Rowan & Littlefield Publishers.

Sowell, Thomas 1983. *The Economics and Politics of Race: An International Perspective*. New York: William Morrow.

Ssu-ma, Ch'ien 1961. *Records of the Grand Historian of China*. Translated from the *Sih Chi* of Ssu-ma Ch'ien. New York: Columbia Univ. Press.

Stein, Ben 1980. *The View from Sunset Boulevard*. Garden City: Anchor Books.

Stewart, Susan 1979. *Nonsense: Aspects of Intertextuality in Folklore and Literature*. Baltimore: Johns Hopkins University Press.

—— 1984. *On Longing: Narratives of the Miniature, the Gigantic, the Souvenir, the Collection*. Johns Hopkins University Press: Baltimore.

Sturdivant, Frederick D. and Vernon-Wrotzel, Heidi 1990. *Business and Society: A Managerial Approach*. Homewood, Ill: Richard D. Irwin, Inc.

Tam, Simon 1990. "Centrifugal Versus Centripetal Growth Processes: Contrasting Ideal Types For Conceptualizing the Developmental Patterns of Chinese and Japanese Firms." In S.R. Clegg and S.G. Gordon, eds. *Capitalism in Contrasting Cultures*. New York: Walter de Gruyter.

Taylor, Charles 1990. "Modes of Civil Society." *Public Culture*, 3, 1: 95–118.

—— 1994. "Can Liberalism be Communitarian? *Critical Review*, 8, 2: 257–62.

Tocqueville, Alexis de [1856] 1968. *Der alte Staat und die Revolution*. Hamburg: Rowohlt.

Tompkins, Jane 1985. *Sensational Designs: The Cultural Work of American Fiction, 1790–1860*. New York: Oxford University Press.

United States Department of Commerce 1998. *Statistical Abstract of the United States*. Washington DC: Bureau of the Census.

Vaughn, Karen I. 1993. *Austrian Economics in America: The Migration of a Tradition*. New York: Cambridge University Press.

Veyne, Paul, ed. 1987. *A History of Private Life: Vol. I. From Pagan Rome to Byzantium*. Cambridge, MA: Harvard University Press.

Villa, Dana R. 1996. *Arendt and Heidegger: The Fate of the Political*. Princeton: Princeton University Press.

Walzer, Michael 1990. "A Critique of Philosophical Conversation." In Michael Kelly, ed. *Hermeneutics and Critical Theory in Ethics and Politics*. Cambridge, MA: The MIT Press: 182–96.

Warnke, Georgia 1987. *Gadamer: Hermeneutics, Tradition and Reason*. Cambridge: Polity Press.

—— 1990a. "Rawls, Habermas, and Real Talk: A Reply to Walzer." In Michael Kelly, ed. *Hermeneutics and Critical Theory in Ethics and Politics*. Cambridge, MA: The MIT Press: 197–203.

—— 1990b. "Social Interpretation and Political Theory: Walzer and His Critics." In Michael Kelly, ed. *Hermeneutics and Critical Theory in Ethics and Politics*. Cambridge, MA: The MIT Press: 204–26.

Warth, Eva-Marie 1994. "'And that's my time.' Soap Opera and the Temporal Organization of Women's Everyday Lives." In Borchers, *et al*. eds. 1994. *Never Ending Stories: American Soap Operas and the Cultural Production of Meaning*. Trier: Wissenschaftlichter Verlag Trier: 216–26.

Weber, Max [1924] 1968. *Economy and Society*. Guenther Roth and Claus Wittich, eds. Originally published as *Wirtschaft und Gesellschaft. Grundriss der verstehenden Soziologie*, 4th ed. Tübingen: Mohr, 1956. Berkeley: University of California Press.

Wellmer, Albrecht 1991. "Models of Freedom in the Modern World." In Michael Kelly, ed. *Hermeneutics and Critical Theory in Ethics and Politics*. Cambridge, MA: The MIT Press: 227–52.

White, Keith 1997. "The Killer App: Wired Magazine, Voice of the Corporate Revolution." In Thomas Frank and Matt Weiland, eds. 1997. *Commodify Your Dissent: Salvos from The Baffler*. New York: W.W. Norton: 46–56.

Wicksteed, Philip 1910 [1933]. *The Common Sense of Political Economy: Selected Papers and Reviews on Economic Theory*. London: Routledge & Sons.

Willis, Paul 1990. *Common Culture: Symbolic Work at Play in the Everyday Cultures of the Young*. Boulder, CO: Westview Press.

Wilson, Clyde, ed. 1981. *Why the South Will Survive*. Atlanta: University of Georgia Press.

Wilson, Tony 1992. *Watching Television: Hermeneutics, Reception, and Popular Culture*. Cambridge: Polity Press.

Wisman, Jon D. 1990. "The Scope and Goals of Economic Science: A Habermasian Perspective." In Don Lavoie, ed. *Economics and Hermeneutics*. New York: Routledge.

Index